A SWINDON HISTORY
1840-1901

By the same author

THE RAILWAY TOWN

A description of life and events in Swindon

from 22 January 1901 to 11 November 1918

Isambard Kingdom Brunel c.1840, from a painting by John Horsley.
His hand rests on a map of the route of the G.W.R.

A
SWINDON HISTORY
1840 - 1901

by
J.SILTO

SALUBRITAS ET INDUSTRIA

SWINDON
1981

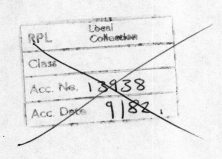
Published by

J.Silto 157 Faringdon Road, Swindon. Wilts.

CONTENTS

CONTENTS

LIST OF ILLUSTRATIONS

INTRODUCTION

The creation of the borough of Swindon, which took place on 9th November 1900, was a joint incorporation of Old and New Swindon, and it brought together under a single municipal administration two communities very diverse in origin and character.

Old Swindon was the result of a long and leisurely growth; a small town built on a hill, set in agricultural country, with some pleasant stone built mansions in its High Street, and holding a market once a week and a one day fair five times a year. There were many such places in early Victorian England and Swindon's only distinction from them was a geological one; the mile long summit of Swindon Hill, upon which the town was built, consisted almost entirely of the famous Portland lime-stone. This feature enabled a quarrying industry to exist alongside the agricultural and market life of the town.

In contrast, New Swindon, at the bottom of the hill, was the creation of the Great Western Railway, and a product of the Industrial Revolution. Here everything was different; the men and navvies imported from all over the country to build or work in the great Locomotive Works seemed to William Morris, Swindon's first historian, to be almost of a different race. He remembers an evening when he watched these navvies trooping into the town through the evening sunlight. 'I stood in The Sands and watched these men ... as I was not half their height, from my point of view their heads and shoulders were thrown right against the heavens .... They appeared to be passing through some palpable material of something which as it was forced aside for their passage, was formed into a variety of layers through which the light from the back penetrated'.[1]

An extravagant fancy, perhaps, but there was in this New Swindon a sense of urgency, of force and impact, that was far removed from that older Swindon community which pursued the even tenor of its way at the top of Swindon Hill.

To bring together these two very different, even opposite groups, was a formidable task and the way in which it was done in sixty crowded years makes a fascinating study. Throughout England Industry was on the march, and the pace of life had quickened, but in Swindon the impact of the Industrial Revolution was so clearly defined and its effect so far reaching that the development of the town between 1840 and 1901 is an almost unique example of the variation in the history of an English town.

Much has been written at length by scholars and writers of repute upon this history.[2] The architecture of the town, its trade, the growth of the Railway Works, the amenities provided by the G.W.R. for its employees, the building of schools, churches and chapels; all these and many other aspects have been catalogued and discussed by authors past and present, and it would be easy to draw from these sources and present a factual and competent history of the town during its years of development.

Such a history, however exhaustive and scholarly, however carefully researched and considered, would yet lack one essential element, an indispensable component that transforms the bare bones of date, place and incident into the flesh and blood of living history. This component is the 'human factor'. A consideration of the "human factor' during this period of Swindon's history poses certain questions. What of the people of the town? What effect did this period of tremendous change have upon them? What did they do in their leisure time? What was life like in the early Railway Village? What were the hopes and fears of the Swindonians who lived during those years? Such questions cannot be answered in a dogmatic or authoritative way but they are not beyond all conjecture.

The present writer has therefore endeavoured to pay particular attention to the lives and habits of the people who lived in the town, to read the papers of their day, to visit the houses in which they lived, even the churchyards where they lie; to study any record of their activities, and to hope, that perhaps fortuitously, he may show them in a new and clearer light.

Notes and References

1. William Morris, "Swindon 50 years ago, more or less" (Swindon 1885) p. 64.

2. Richard Jefferies gives a vivid account of the G.W.R. Swindon Works in 1867, in his "Jefferies Land. A History of Swindon and its Environs." (edited by Grace Toplis and published in London in 1896.

   Frederick Large in his "Swindon Retrospect" (Swindon 1892) describes the town and its personalities as he knew them in mid-Victorian days.

   A more detailed and informative work which includes a chapter on the architecture of Swindon, is "Studies in the History of Swindon" by L.V. Grinsell, H.B. Wells, H.S. Tallamy and John Betjeman. (Swindon Borough Council 1950).

   "The Victoria County History of Wilts" (Oxford University Press, London, 1970) is an authoritative work on the history of Swindon and the surrounding towns.

CHAPTER 1

SWINDON IN 1840, AND THE COMING OF THE RAILWAY

'The town is situated on the summit of a hill
of considerable eminence, which commands a
delightful view of parts of Berkshire and
Gloucestershire. The principal streets are
wide and contain many good houses. No particular manufacture is carried on in the town,
but it is the residence of many persons of
independent fortune. Extensive quarries are
wrought in the neighbourhood, which, together
with agricultural pursuits, afford employment
to the greater part of the working population
of the town. The inhabitants are abundantly
supplied with pure water from springs. There
are 325 houses in the town and the population
at the 1831 census was 1742.'

This description of Swindon appeared in an 1840 Gazetteer,[1] and the
principal street - High Street - was, indeed, pleasant and residential, with fine houses built of limestone, 'where lived a number of
people in easy circumstances.'[2] Here, too, were the principal inns
of the town: the "Goddard Arms", a mid-eighteenth century building
of brick, with a long frontage of nine bays and a stone tiled roof,
and the "Bell", a posting house reputed to date from 1515.[3]
Opposite the "Goddard Arms" was the "King of Prussia", which
commanded a large amount of patronage on fair days, when the
assembly room was turned into a temporary ballroom and dancing
continued 'fast and furious for many hours to the strains of a
violin, played by a travelling gypsy, whose music was limited to
one tune all day.'[4]

On the east side of the street two stately pillars, or gatepiers,
each flanked by a small lodge, marked the entrance to a pleasant tree
lined avenue, leading to a broad and spacious park. From the high
ground of the park a fine view of the surrounding countryside could
be obtained. As far as the eye could see the scene was almost
completely rural; field and wood rolled away into the distance, and
the only signs of human habitation were a few isolated cottages, the
more remote of which only indicated their presence by the curling

wisps of wood smoke climbing lazily from their chimneys. To the south
the view was different, for in that direction the park sloped gently
down to softer ground, where clear spring water bubbled through, and
two small lakes gave variety to the universal greenery. In the
distance was the impressive background of the immutable Downs.

In the park were two buildings - an elegant brick and stone manor
house, and an old English country church. The house - known as "The
Lawn" - was the family home of the Goddards, a family of ancient lineage,
whose connection with Swindon could be traced back to 1404. This
notable family had been hereditary Lords of the Manor of Swindon since
1563, when Thomas Goddard 'had acquired the manors of Over and Nether
Swindon, together with fairs and markets, and appurtenances including
two watermills'.[5] In 1840 the Lord of the Manor was 61 year old
Ambrose Goddard Esq., Member of Parliament for the Cricklade Division
of Wiltshire, head of the Goddard family, and chief landowner of the
town. He had married at 40, and his son, Ambrose Lethbridge Goddard,
was completing his Harrow and Cambridge education before returning to
help in the running of the extensive family estate.

The church was that of Holy Rood - the parish church of Swindon.
It was a typical old English church, with a squat square tower;
surrounded by a high brick wall often in need of repair, against which,
on the southern side was a large pond. First built in 1154, it had
been restored and repaired so often in the ensuing centuries, that by
1840 little was left of the original church. Every Sunday the
prominent citizens of the town - the Goddards, the Bradfords, the
Viletts, Noads, Hardings and others made their way to their allotted
pews in the crowded church.

Further down High Street was the Market Square, where every Monday
the local farmers, tradesmen, cattle dealers, pedlars, cheapjacks and
others jostled together in an atmosphere of agitation and excitement.
The local inns were crowded with thirsty customers, two of the busiest
being the "Bull" in Newport Street, and "The Bell and Shoulder of
Mutton" at the bottom of High Street. The south side of the Market
Square was occupied with a long low building of stables with lofts
above. In these stables were kept the horses for the London stage

coach, which left the "Bell" three times weekly for London, taking about ten hours on the journey and returning the following day. Two other stage coaches included Swindon in their routes. One made Swindon a daily stage in its journey from Oxford to Bath, and the other travelled to Cheltenham from Southampton by way of Swindon. The "Bell" was an important Swindon hostelry, and was to remain so until the advent of the railway quickly brought stage coach travel to a close. Even then it would adjust to the change, as it had done before in its long history. The "Bell" had a Flemish tradition, as, indeed, had other parts of the town, for many refugees from the Low Countries had settled in the Swindon area during the 15th and 16th centuries.

Turning west from High Street was Newport Street, the home of many of the smaller tradesmen of the town. It consisted chiefly of thatched and whitewashed cottages, and was often called "Bull" Street, from the public house of that sign, situated half way along the street. Here, too, was the National School, rebuilt in 1835, and Tarrant, the boot and shoe maker, whose business had been there since 1814. Henry Tarrant was the Town Constable, responsible for the billeting of troops, for the regulation of the stalls in the Market Place and the polling arrangements. He was also in charge of the Stocks and the Cattle Pound.[6] Sanitation and drainage left much to be desired in Newport Street, as it did in the rest of the town. Footpaths needed repair, rubbish and filth was regularly deposited on the street, and cess pits were the only form of sewage disposal.

Short Hedge, as Devizes Road was then called, led north from Newport Street, and was chiefly notable for the horse sales that were held there every Monday, the horses being tethered to the trees and hedges that lined the street. A few cattle and horse pens had been constructed for this trade, and offices of a sort provided for the auctioneers and the buyers to do their business. Approaching the end of Short Hedge were a few simple houses known as Bath Buildings.

Wood Street contained a number of thatched cottages, but there were also several small businesses; one of the most prominent being that of Blackford the butcher, whose shop was on the corner of Wood Street and Cricklade Street. Robert Blackford of this family was well known in the town because of his ability as a 'backsword' player. Backswords or singlesticks, was a popular sport of the time, and matches involving prize money and side bets were often arranged. It was certainly not a game for those of a gentle disposition, for each player was armed with a stout ash cudgel, and the play consisted of seeking an opening to bring the cudgel down on the opponent's head and 'be first to let blood'. 'Kicking the shins' was also an acceptable ploy.[7]

Cricklade Street entered the town from the north by way of a steep hill, which in icy weather offered a real hazard for the stage coaches. A few cottages and small houses lined the street as it approached the town and one house was quite outstanding. This was known as "The Hall", and was a house of brick and stone of graceful proportion and arrangement. It had been built in 1729 by the Harding family, who owned considerable land and property at the bottom of Swindon Hill. Later it passed to the Sheppard family, and is now No. 42 Cricklade Street, the offices of Townsends, the solicitors.

Other building in the town included Brittania Place, a small street of cottages leading off Short Hedge, built in 1818, and The Planks, a few stone built cottages from Market Square to Old Mill Lane. Here the road was often muddy, and a raised walkway was built and called 'The Planks'. 'The Sands', (now Bath Road), was a rural path leading to Okus and the quarries. Apsley House, (now the Museum), had been built for the Toomer family, and on the same side of the Sands were three brick houses, 'plain two storied units with projecting eaves, low pitched roofs and singularly attractive trellised porches, each of a different design'.[8]

At the foot of Swindon Hill, where New Swindon was to grow, was farmland and on it stood 'hundreds of fine old elms and other trees'.[9] The only break in the vista of pasture land was the thin ribbon of the Wilts and Berks Canal, which ran from the Bristol Avon valley through Melksham, Chippenham, Calne, Swindon, Wantage to Abingdon and the Thames.

The canal, which had been completed in 1818, was principally used to carry coal from the South Gloucestershire and North Somerset coal-fields. For Swindon, however, its main contribution was to carry stone from the Swindon quarries to the surrounding towns, where it found a ready sale. This stone was also used extensively for the building of bridges and in other works of the canal. The presence of the canal also influenced a decision that was to revolutionise the development of the town. Another Swindon connection with the canal was that the chairman of the Canal Company was Ambrose Goddard, of "The Lawn", Swindon.

Technical consideration of locks and water levels made it necessary that a reservoir of water should be available near Swindon, and after an abortive attempt to sink a deep well that would release enough water to form a reservoir at Westcott Place, it was decided to construct Coate Water. Skating at Coate and on the canal was a popular pastime during the severe winters of the time.

Like other hill top towns Swindon had its share of convergent roads; three, from Cricklade, Highworth and Faringdon entered from the North; one, from Wootton Bassett and Malmesbury, from the West; and two, from Devizes and Marlborough, from the South. It was not an important road centre, however, and Swindon was no better placed to attract growth than many similar towns through-out the country. Its progress might have been that of another Chippenham or Highworth, except for one very important circumstance. The Railway Age had begun and the Great Western Railway was building its main line from London to Bristol. The original plan was that it should follow the old coach road through the Vale of Pewsey, but owing to strong opposition from the local landed gentry this scheme was abandoned, and an alternative route through the low ground at the northern edge of the Wiltshire Downs chosen. The Engineer to the Company was the 30 year old Isambard Kingdom Brunel, destined to become one of the most famous of all engineers. Brunel appointed as his Superintendent of Locomotives Daniel Gooch, a young man who scarcely reached his majority; he was to hold the position for the next 27 years, during which time he was to be knighted for his services. As the line grew, even before it reached Swindon, the town was very much in the thoughts of these two young men, for, with the rapid growth of the railway, they realised the necessity for the provision of a central repair depot for the maintenance of the locomotive stock. The youthful Mr. Gooch was asked to investigate and report on the most desirable location for such a depot. In his diary he wrote:

'1840. During this year, further portions of the Great Western were opened and agreements were made for leasing the Bristol and Exeter and the Swindon and Cheltenham Railways, and it became necessary to furnish a large Works for the repair etc., of our stock. I was called upon to report on the best situation to build these Works, and on full consideration, I reported in favour of Swindon, it being the junction with the Cheltenham branch and also a convenient division of the Great Western Line for the engine working. Mr. Brunel and I went to look at the ground, then only green fields, and he agreed with me as to its being the best place'.

It has gone down in Swindon folk lore that the actual site of the first building was decided by either Brunel or Gooch throwing a stone, or, in some versions, a sandwich from their picnic lunch, into the air, and then marking the spot. The throwing of stones, swords and other articles is, however, not an uncommon method of site choosing in mythology, and there does not appear to be any reliable evidence that verifies such an incident. It cannot be said, however, that the historic meeting lacked drama, and Richard Jefferies in his book "The Hills and the Vales" describes the scene:

'.... a certain party of gentlemen sat down to luncheon on the greensward, which was then where the platform is now. The furze was in blossom around them, the rabbits frisked in and out of their burrows; two or three distant farmhouses, one or two cottages, these were all the signs of human habitation, except a few cart tracks, indicating a track used for field purposes. Then these gentlemen lunched, and one among them, ay, two among them, meditated great things, which the first planned, and the second lived to see realise the most sanguine anticipations. These two gentlemen were Isambard Kingdom Brunel and Daniel Gooch....'

One can visualise the two dark suited young Victorians, Brunel with his stove pipe hat and inevitable cheroot, Gooch alert and towering in

the confidence of his 23 years; watch their grave discussion of the
merits and demerits of the site, and mark the final approving nod of
agreement. Around them 'only green fields', and the only sound that
of the crows in 'the fine old elms'. In such a setting was the
momentous decision taken.

The technical considerations of the choice were: Gradients on the
line determined the site of the junction with the Cheltenham railway,
and the configuration of the ground also led to a meeting at this
spot with the Wilts and Berks Canal, affording direct connection with
the Somerset coalfields. The canal and its reservoir at Coate would
also serve in the last resort as a water supply. Swindon was
convenient for the necessary changing of engines, due to one type of
locomotive pulling the trains along the easy gradients from London,
and another continuing the journey across the hills to Bath and
Bristol. Nearby was the Wootton Bassett incline which was thought
to demand a ready stock of banking engines to assist the ascent.

The recommendation that Swindon should be chosen as the site of
the Works was endorsed by the Directors of the Company who decided

> 'to provide an Engine Establishment at Swindon,
> commensurate with the wants of the Company, where a
> change of engines may be advantageously made, and the
> trains stopped for the purpose of Passengers taking
> refreshment as is the case at Wolverton on the London
> to Birmingham Railway. The Establishment there would
> also comprehend the large repairing shops for the
> Locomotive Department, and this circumstance rendered
> it necessary to arrange for the building of Cottages
> etc., for the residence of many persons employed in
> the service of the Company.'[10]

On 16th December 1840 the line reached Swindon, and by June 1841
the whole line from London to Bristol, including Box Tunnel, was in
use. At Swindon there was almost feverish activity, for, in the
early railway days, decisions, once taken, were quickly implemented.
Plans to build 300 cottages were made. Land was bought and work
began on the building of the Locomotive Works and the Railway Village.
The development of Swindon as a Railway Town had commenced.

Notes and references

1. The Parliamentary Gazetteer of England and Wales 1840-1843 A. Fullerton & Co. London 1843.

2. J. Robson. A Commercial Directory of Wilts (1838).

3. Inscription on building.

4. F. Large A Swindon Retrospect p. 36

5. Swindon Studies p. 29

6. Information taken from a copy of the 'recollection of Old Swindon' dictated by Richard Tarrant (1840-1926), formerly of Wood Street, Swindon. I am indebted to Mr. A.P. Lenham of Swindon for the loan of these notes.

7. W. Morris. Swindon 50 years ago p. 129. Some of Robert Blackford's descendants still live in the town.

8. John Betjeman in Swindon Studies p. 163

9. F. Large. A Swindon Retrospect p. 120

10. E.T. McDermott. A History of the GWR Vol. 2. pp. 120-1.

CHAPTER 2

THE IMPACT OF THE RAILWAY 1841-1851

The focal point of New Swindon was the railway station, which was
opened in July 1842.[1] It consisted of two plain Georgian style
blocks, one on each side of the line, and was more functional than
ornamental. It was certainly durable, for the main building remained
practically unchanged until July 1972, when the rebuilding and
modernization of the station commenced.[2] All trains stopped at
Swindon for ten minutes 'for the purpose of the Passengers taking
refreshment', and dining and refreshment rooms were provided. By a
curious arrangement the cost of providing these facilities was borne
by the builders of the station - Messrs. J. and C. Rigby of Millbank,
London. In return they were granted a 99 year lease of the premises,
and in turn, sublet them to a Cheltenham hotelier, whose high prices
and inferior quality food soon came in for strong criticism from the
travelling public.

To reach the station travellers from Old Swindon made their way
by an old road that led from Swindon Hill to the 'Golden Lion'
bridge[3] of the Wilts and Berks canal, and from there, by a cinder
track across fields, which brought them out opposite the station.
To get to the booking office it was necessary to climb a steep slope,
which in wet and slippery weather was only accomplished with great
difficulty.[4] A small hotel - the "Queens Hotel" - had been built at
the same time as the station, and apart from this, and a few isolated
station outbuildings, the whole situation was rural.

However, a half mile to the west, work had commenced on the
building of the Locomotive Works, and also on the Railway Village,
which was to provide living accommodation for the railway workers
and their families. This Railway Village was thought to have been
designed by Sir Matthew Digby Wyatt, the architect of Paddington
Station, and for many years it has been of great interest to
builders and architects. It must be one of the earliest experiments

in planned industrial building in Great Britain.

The estate was laid out on a symmetrical plan about a central square, originally called High Street. The fact that there was also a High Street in Old Swindon does not seem to have caused any confusion, and it was not until many years after that the street was renamed Emlyn Square, after Viscount Emlyn, a chairman of the G.W.R. From the west and east sides of High Street ran four parallel streets. These streets were named after stations on the line, the western ones being Bristol, Bath (later renamed Bathampton), Exeter and Taunton Streets[5], and the eastern ones being London, Reading, Oxford and Faringdon Streets. Although small by modern standards, the houses were sturdily built of local stone and attractively designed. In general their style followed the Georgian tradition, but the facades facing London Street and Bristol Street were embellished by small gables. Each house had a small front garden facing a wide street, and a yard at the rear containing a wash house and a privy; back alleys gave access to the yards. The houses have now been modernized, but the exteriors have not been altered and stand as a tribute to the ability and style of the designers. John Betjeman, in his study of the architecture of Swindon, states that the whole effect must have been 'spacious and delightful'.[6]

The spiritual, educational and physical welfare of the Company's employees had not been neglected in the scheme. A director of the Company, C.H. Gibbs, who died in 1842, left £500 towards the cost of building a church and a school. The Company appealed for further funds, and found the response was so good that the church (St. Marks), costing £6,000, and the school were completed in 1845. A plot of land between the church and Faringdon Road was purchased for use as a park and sports field, and this completed the planned scheme.

The layout of the estate has been vividly preserved by a painting which can be seen in the Swindon Railway Museum.[8] It gives a bird's eye view of the New Town scene, and amongst other things throws an interesting light on the ways in which the children of the estate amused themselves. We see two of them sparring up to each other in prize fighting attitudes, others appear to be playing the old game of 'Tag', and there is also a Maypole, with children hanging from ropes and

Swindon Station, 1845

New Swindon in 1849. by *Edward Snell.*

The Engine House at Swindon Works c.1850

whirling around the pole. A cricket match is in progress on 'The Park', and the batsmen are shown moving between the wickets, whilst the bowler waits for the ball to be returned, and one is reminded of Francis Thompson's 'run getters flickering to and fro', as the painting portrays New Swindon's equivalents of 'Hornby and Barlow long ago'.[9]

'The Park' occupies a special place in the history of Swindon. In the early days of the developing town it was the natural leisure place for the people of the Railway Village - young anf old. It was also a continuing amenity. The boy who joined his young companions there at play, and ran and jumped to his heart's content, found that as he grew into early manhood, and took his place as a worker in the ever growing Works, that The Park was the place to meet his mates in the summer evenings after work; to laugh and joke with them, and perhaps to catch the eyes of one of the demure young ladies walking sedately with her friends. A few years later he could take his wife and children there for a modest picnic 'Tea in The Park', and as the inexorable years rolled on, The Park could still offer him, as an old man, a look at a cricket match, a seat in the sun, and a view of the broad gauge expresses puffing along the nearby main line.

Also shown in the picture is the Locomotive Works - an embryo of the huge complex it was to become. Scenes of activity are shown; the main lifting device seems to be the tripod and block and tackle, and the wheel shop with its stock of spare wheels seems to be a major shop, easily recognisable in the foreground. Six tall factory chimneys are sending clouds of smoke over the countryside, which rolls away into the distance, and miniature trains move along the Gloucester branch line. The workmen on the sidings wear beards and rough woolly hats; they look strong, hard men and one begins to understand William Morris's description of them as he watched them trooping into the town.

Thw Railway Company was aware of its obligations to its employees and one of its most enlightened schemes was the 'G.W.R. Medical Fund Society', founded in 1847.[10] By this scheme medical care for the employee and his family was provided, in return for a small weekly subscription deducted from his wages.

The cultural and leisure needs of the men were not neglected. With the approval of the Directors a 'Mechanics Institute' was formed, with the object of 'disseminating useful knowledge and encouraging rational amusement amongst all classes of people employed by the Company at Swindon.' This started in a modest way in January 1844, with 15 members and a library of 150 books. By the end of the year the membership had increased to 129, and the books numbered 522, and were on loan at the rate of 80 each week.[11] All activities took place in the Works; one of the main engineering shops being used for lectures and discussions, whilst dancing and amusements were held in the paint shop.

In 1849 the Company granted their employees an annual day excursion which soon became known as 'Trip', an event that became an integral part of the social life of the railway community. All employees could join Provident Societies, which made provision for sickness and old age benefits. The G.W.R. Provident Society was formed as early as 1838, and the Locomotive Department Sick Fund in 1843. Thrift was encouraged amongst the staff, and for this purpose the G.W.R. formed its own Savings Bank, where men could have part of their pay paid into their accounts.

By 1848 the establishment at the Works had risen to 1,800 and the Railway Village began to be seriously overcrowded. Further housing became essential. To meet the need, a considerable area of working class housing was built on the line of the 'Fleetway' track which ran roughly parallel to the main line and the Wilts and Berks Canal, and about half way between the two. These long terraces of houses lined the western approaches to the town, the main street being called Westcott Place. They were not such pleasant houses as those on the railway estate and lacked character and style. Overcrowding in New Swindon remained a problem for the new few years, and in some cases when the 'night men got up, the day men went to bed', and workers were leaving Swindon because they could not find a place to live.[12]

Other disquieting features accompanied the early development of the town. The average age at death had gone down from over 36 in 1820-29 to under 30 in 1840-49.[13] This appalling figure must be considered in conjunction with the infant mortality rate in early Victorian England. The water supply, except for that in the Railway Village, was suspect, and the local wells were often contaminated. The only form of sewage disposal was by cess pits. Street rubbish and storm water was conveyed by gutters into covered drains which emptied outside the town. These often became blocked and offensive. The Railway Village was inspected monthly by G.W.R. housing inspectors, who ensured that the houses were kept clean and tidy. Free issues of lime for cleaning and disinfecting were always available. Even so, there was an out-break of smallpox in the Village in 1847-48.[14]

There was so much concern in the town over the situation that in 1849 162 prominent citizens of Old Swindon petitioned the Board of Health, asking for an inquiry into the sanitary conditions of the town. As a result, an official of the Board - Inspector S.J. Clark - carried out an inspection in the following year. His findings were confined to Old Swindon and recommended a) Provision of a sewage system b) A piped water supply c) The formation of Local Boards in accordance with the Public Health Act.[15] These desirable recommend-ations were not to be fully carried out for some years. The two towns were not ready for them, or their cost, and in the meantime the worst of the problems were dealt with by other means.

There was very little co-operation between the two communities at this time. The people of Old Town viewed New Town with a certain amount of apprehension and thought that many of the people living there were rough and uncouth. Undoubtedly, the influx of hundreds of navvies and labourers to work on the Works and the permanent way had caused a lot of drunkenness in the New Town. On the other hand, the business community of Old Town welcomed the trade the newcomers brought with them.

One can conjecture, perhaps, on the thoughts of some of the people of Old Town in 1850. Ambrose Goddard, the Lord of the Manor, and Colonel Vilett, the main landowners, must have thought that the coming of the railway would increase the value of their land, offering dividends far beyond those they received from their tenant farmers. Deacon, the clock and watchmaker, in Wood Street, Blackford the butcher on the corner of Wood Street and Cricklade Street, and Reynolds, the leather merchant, must have realised that increased trade would result from the rapid growth of the town consequent on the arrival of the railway and the building of the Locomotive Works. Men with drive and vision realised that it was a time of opportunity and began to start businesses. One of the first of these was John Arkell, who as early as 1843 began a brewing business at Kingsdown, and founded a firm that was to become the principal brewery of the town.

Opportunity, however, was more limited for the workers in the Railway Works. Discipline was severe and the hours long and arduous. Work in a factory making locomotives has never been an easy task; the nature of the undertaking prevents it being carried out in quiet, airy surroundings, and in the early days it must have been an ordeal. Mechnical appliances were not so plentiful as they are now. Riveting, for example, needed a team of three - a 'striker', with a sledgehammer, a 'holder up', who held the rivets with tongs for the 'striker', and some unfortunate boy, the 'rivet hotter', who had the job of heating the rivets to nearly white heat, and spent most of his working day crouched over a coke fire, which he maintained at the right degree of heat by the use of bellows and the judicious feeding of fuel.

The noise, heat and general harshness of the work, together with the overcrowding in the houses, had their effect on the health of the less robust of the employees.

Notes and references

1. Swindon Station was the summit of the G.W.R. main line, being 270 feet above Paddington Station and 292 feet above Bristol.

2. The Hambro Life building now dominates the Station area.

3. Large. A Swindon Retrospect. p. 17

4. Ibid. p. 18

5. Bath Street was altered to Bathampton Street in order to avoid confusion with Bath Road in Old Town.

6. Swindon Studies p. 102

7. Ibid. p. 111

8. "New Swindon" by Edward Snell. Swindon Railway Museum.

9. "At Lord's" from the Collected Poems of Francis Thompson (Oxford University Press) 1932.

10. Swindon Studies p. 115

11. Railway Gazette 15th October 1943

12. V.C.H. Wilts IX p. 128

13. Swindon Studies p. 102

14. Ibid.

15. G.T. Clark "Report to the Board of Health on Swindon (1851)".

CHAPTER 3

THE DEVELOPMENT OF THE TOWN

The decade 1851-1861 was one of great expansion in the Works. The population of New Town increased rapidly, and overcrowding continued to be the principal problem. The Railway Village, Westcott Place and the small groups of houses near the station and the canal bridges could not cope with the influx of workers, many of whom were forced to find accommodation in the nearby villages and small towns. The Company ran special workmens' trains for these employees, and as work started at 6 a.m. and finished at 6 p.m. their leisure time must have been limited. A large Company building in Faringdon Street was converted into a 100 bed hostel for unmarried men. It was known as "The Barracks', and was useful as a temporary measure. By 1867 it was no longer in use, and became a Methodist church, remaining as such for many years. Since 1962 it has been the Swindon Railway Museum.

More housing was essential and private building began near the Works. Most of this was in the Fleetway (Fleet Street) - Bridge Street - Golden Lion Bridge area. The Golden Lion Bridge (built 1806) crossed the Wilts and Berks Canal, and was so called because of the nearby 'Golden Lion' public house, the sign of which was a magnificent stone Golden Lion couchant, at that time over the entrance to the inn, but in later years reating on a plinth in the forecourt. By 1861 the settlement had grown considerably, and small terraces of houses and cottages had appeared. Shops began to open, and in 1861 were listed[1] as being in Fleet Street, Canal Walk, Bridge Road and Alma Terrace. On the south side of the canal were Hope Cottages, Crimea Cottages, Mount Pleasant and Barnes Cottages.

Between 1861 and 1871 Bridge Street became the shopping centre for the New Town, 'with shops and houses in abundance, 3 places of worship, a Methodist chapel, a Roman Catholic chapel and a Free Christian Church, and no less than 7 public houses'. Other areas of

development were in the East Street and Church Place districts of the
Railway Village, and on a field called 'Road Ground', immediately to
the east of the Railway Village. Three streets were built here. At
first they were regarded as part of London, Oxford and Reading Streets,
but in 1870 John Harding Sheppard, who had owned the field, modestly
requested that they should be called Sheppard, Harding and John Streets
and this was done. However, 'John Street' was always known as 'Henry
Street', probably as a John Street, south of Fleet Street already
existed.[2]

Between 1861 and 1871 the most important building in the New Town
was along the lane from Eastcott to the Golden Lion bridge, and then
north via Bridge Street to the "Union Railway Inn". This is now the
line of Regent Street and Bridge Street, and the chief shopping centre
of the town. The "Union Railway Inn" was situated on the northern
side of the Bridge Street - Station Road junction. It was a prominent
public house in Victorian Swindon and was connected with the North
Wilts Canal trade. Bullins Bridge, which crossed the nearby canal,
was so called because the licensee of the "Union Railway Inn" at the
time was one Bullin, who originated from Wantage.

Many Welshmen had come to Swindon to work in the Works, mostly in
the Rail Mill, and to provide accommodation for them and their
families the stone fronted cottages of Cambria Place were built in
the Westcott Place area in the early 1860's. Other building began
in the Cromwell, Brunel and Havelock Streets areas (1867), in
Gloucester, Cheltenham and Wellington Streets (1869), and Rolleston,
Byron, Dover, Western and North Streets (1869).

The fields that were shown surrounding the Works in Snell's
picture of Swindon in 1849 had disappeared one by one as the town
grew, not without their owners making a handsome profit on their
sale. It was said that

> 'land which was scarcely worth the trouble of
> attending to, much of it covered with furze, the
> retreat of rabbits and game, and a playground for
> boys, was purchased at a price equal to that given
> for the best in other situations.'[3]

New Swindon changed from a working class suburb into a town in its

Mechanics' Institution, 1855

An old photograph (c. 1880) of New Swindon, taken
from Gilbert's Hill, before the development of the
Commercial Road area. 'The Barracks', now the
Railway Museum, is the turreted building in the
left background with Farnsby Street leading to it.

own right. The inhabitants of the town were proud of its rapid
development and obviously felt that it was destined to be 'no
mean city'. This growth of civic pride is shown by the editor of
a local directory for 1878.[4] Writing of the events of the previous
year he tells his readers that:

> 'It is no exaggeration to say that 1877 has witnessed
> an advance in New Swindon beyond anticipation. The
> growth of houses has been astonishing, many scores
> have been erected during the year, whilst month by
> month the Local Board sanctions further erections.
> There has also been a corresponding development of
> existing resources - old buildings having been extended,
> renovated or varied until it may be truly said that
> few, if any, towns similar to New Swindon are better
> supplied with commodious and attractive shops and
> places of business. The town has also improved,
> paving, road making and other permanent works have
> been carried out and further operations are in
> contemplation. Originally dependent on the artisan
> population in the employ of the G.W.R. Company, New
> Swindon shopkeepers, though undoubtedly owing much
> to the support of the work people, find in the other
> industries of the place, the number of men employed
> in building etc., a new class of customer. In other
> words, the town is growing, its central position and
> railway facilities attracting trade and manufactures.'

By January 1878 the town consisted of the following streets:

Old Swindon

Albert Street
Avenue Road
Back Lane
Bath Buildings
Bath Road
Broome Tythings
Belle Vue Road
Brittania Place
Cricklade Street
Dammas Lane
Devizes Road
Eastcott Lane
High Street
King John Street
King William Street
Lansdown Road
Marlborough Road
Market Square
Newport Street
North Street
Prospect Lane

New Swindon

Albion Cottages
Bath Street
Bridge Street
Bristol Street
Brunel Street
Byron Street
Cambria Houses
Cambria Place
Canal Street
Catherine Street
Cetus Buildings
Carfax Street
Carr Street
Cheltenham Street
Church Place
Clarendon Gardens
Cow Lane
Cromwell Street
Dixon Street
Dover Street
East Street

Eastcott Hill
Exeter Street
Falcon Terrace
Faringdon Street
Farnsby Street
Fleet Street
Gladstone Street
Gloucester Street
Gloucester Terrace
Gooch Street
Harding Street
Havelock Street
Hay Lane (Eastcott)
Haydon Street
Henry Street
High Street
Holbrook Street
John Street
King Street
Ladds Mill
Lamb Terrace

Old Swindon

Malthouse Cottages
South Street
The Quarries
Union Row
Union Street
Victoria Street
Victoria Street (North)
Wood Street

New Swindon

Linslade Street
London Street
Merton Street
Mill Street
North Street
Oriel Street
Oxford Street
Prospect Hill
Queen Street
Reading Street
Regent Street
Rodbourne Road
Rolleston Street

Sheppard Street
Stafford Street
Station Road
Taunton Street
Turl Street
Vilett Street
Wellington Street
Westcott Place
Westcott Street
Western Street
Weymouth Street
York Place

Some of the streets were not fully built up - Avenue Road, for example, had no more than three houses - but, in such cases, building continued and the streets gradually grew.

Between 1878 and 1881 there was a slight pause in the building boom. There was a general industrial and agricultural depression, and this was reflected in the traffic receipts of the G.W.R. However, the main factor hampering the development of Swindon New Town was not the trade depression, which soon cleared up, but the difficulty in obtaining land on which to build the much needed houses. Particularly was this so in the area to the west of the town, where the large estates of the old Vilett family[5] were involved in a long and involved suit in chancery, and could only with difficulty be offered for sale by the trustees. This was an extensive area, bounded by Faringdon Road - Regent Street - Dixon Street, strategically placed for the future development of the town. In 1885 the law suit was finally settled, and the land became available for sale to the waiting builders. Tentative plans for its development had already been made. Commercial Road, running from the bottom of Eastcott Hill direct to Faringdon Road and the Railway Village, was the main thoroughfare. Cromby Street and Curtis Street were important streets in the new development, and a network of side streets ran from them. Within the next few years hundreds of terraced houses appeared. They were sturdy and utilitarian, rather than ornate, and only Milton Road (as the northern half of Commercial Road was named) possessed three storied buildings. A Market was built in Commercial Road in 1892.

The opening up of the Commercial Road district was the start of a building boom such as the town had never before experienced. Between 1881 and 1901 the population of Swindon more than doubled, and housing for the newcomers had to be found. In all areas of the town the built up areas increased; the town could be seen to grow from day to day. The estate containing Ashford, Kent, Hythe, Maidstone and Folkestone Roads was complete by 1899, and so were several streets north of Kingshill. In the Westcott area Dean and Birch Streets and their connecting streets were built up. Park Lane was completed.

Another important development was at Rodbourne, where streets were built to the east and west of Rodbourne Road, and a new suburb created. Gorse Hill was well built up by 1900, and so were Florence, Whiteman, Poulton and Beatrice Streets. In the Eastcott area the farm track from the Whale Bridge over the canal to Lower Eastcott was made into Corporation Street, and east of it several streets were laid out, stretching from the partly built Manchester Road to Volta Road.

In the centre of the town, at the junction of Commercial Road, Regent Street and Eastcott Hill, a square shaped open area was formed and developed. This was Regent Circus, and it was here that the council offices were built. This building was the Town Hall – for many years the most prominent secular building in Swindon. John Betjeman refers to it as a 'kind of Danish Renaissance style of brick and stone', and describes its 'domes and adornments'.[6] It was, however, by any standards, the land-mark of New Swindon, with its high tower and four faced clock, dominating the approach from Regent Street. From its balcony the parliamentary election results were declared, and although it no longer houses the civic offices, it still remains the 'Town Hall' to Swindonians. It would be hard to mistake it for anything else.

Since 1865, Regent Street had grown into the main shopping street of the town, crowded with shoppers and bystanders, whose only traffic problem was to avoid the occasional horse and cart. Victoria Road, the natural route from Old Town to New Town, had spread from the original Victoria Street to Victoria Street North, and down the hill to Regent Circus. By 1888 it was made up, and considerably built up by 1899. By the 1890's several well built up streets ran from it on both sides.

Old Town had also shared in the general expansion of the town. Avenue Road, Springfield Road and Lethbridge Road were all laid out and building commenced by 1885, and by 1900 building had commenced on Goddard Avenue, Saint Margaret's Road, Winifred Street and Okus and Westlecot Roads. However, Old Town still retained its residential appearance, and there was none of the over building that occurred in parts of New Swindon.

The provision of parks and playing fields was not forgotten in the rush of development, and in 1894 the Old Swindon Board made provision for the Town Gardens,[7] to be built on a seven acre plot of land near the old Okus quarries. This was an inspired choice of site, lending itself to development and set high above the industrial part of the town. The ground was carefully and artistically laid out, with pleasant tree lined walks and lawns bordered with masses of flowers. The music from the Victorian bandstand, the laughter from the children lost in the Maze, the beautiful and brilliantly coloured peacock strutting across the carefully trimmed grass were a few of the sights and sounds that brought pleasure to the Swindonians who visited the 'Town Gardens'.

The Wilts County Ground, the famous headquarters of the Swindon Town Football and Cricket Clubs was opened in May 1893, and recreation grounds were provided at Rodbourne, Birch Street, Gorse Hill and Cambria Bridge Road.

Notes and references

1. Moore's Almanack 1861

2. V.C.H. Wilts IX p. 111

3. R. Jefferies Jefferies Land p. 63

4. Swindon and District Directory 1878

5. These had become the property of Colonel W.V. Rolleston.

6. Swindon Studies p. 181

7. Old Swindon Local Board Minute Book 1894

CHAPTER 4

_____

LOCAL GOVERNMENT AND THE CREATION OF THE BOROUGH

In the late 1840's and early 1850's the main problem for the local
authorities was sanitation. Clark's report brought no immediate
improvement, and in June 1856 the 'Swindon Advertiser' complained
'that the death rate in the town is 40 per 1000, or double what it
ought to be, and that Inspector Clark's report was a very tame
affair, full of palpable blunders'.[1] The Nuisance Removal Act of
1855 granted to the local authority

> 'full powers to act in all cases of unwholesome or
> crowded dwellings, bad drainage, offensive accumulations,
> unfit or unwholesome food, foul ditches, drains and
> sewers and all other things of a like nature'.

A 'Swindon Nuisance Removal Committee' was set up, and a
'Presentment Book', in which the inhabitants could report any
nuisance, was held at the offices of the Committee. In October
1856 the Committee reported that it had authorized the construction
of

> 'a new sewer, to commence at a point opposite The
> Greyhound Inn, to the Baptist Chapel, thence,
> passing underneath the Canal at the 'Golden Lion',
> to Mr. Reynold's house at Eastcott, at 6s.9d. a
> yard. To Mr. Joseph Barnes of Dauntsey, a contract
> for draining that part of New Swindon that does not
> belong to the G.W.R. Company.'[2]

In 1857 sewers were constructed in Newport Street, Bridge
Street, High Street and Wood Street. A firm of Surveyors was
asked to draw up drainage plans for the town. Action was taken
against public health offenders and in March 1860 a charge was
laid against the landlord of the 'King of Prussia', for allowing
'the privies of the Inn to be in a broken and unwholesome
condition'. As the landlord was advertising 'appetising and
wholesome meals' at the time, such action was undoubtedly
justified. Sewage disposal facilities were unsatisfactory for

some years and as late as 1865 a letter signed 'Ratepayer' appeared in the 'Advertiser'[3] complaining:

> 'with small pox and fever raging in the town as it never raged before, the sewage collectors removing the night soil from Wood Street left a large quantity on the street, where it remained all day, with merely a sprinkling of sand on it.'

In 1871 new and more efficient sewers were laid in the town. A farm of 108 acres at Rodbourne Cheney was bought for £7,750 and laid out as a sewage farm. By 1880 there was a great improvement, although outbreaks of typhoid occurred in September of that year, and the Medical Officer found in necessary for the 'sewers to be flushed with Carbolic Acid.'

The general dissatisfaction with sanitation in the early days of Swindon applied particularly to the water supply, which, apart from the Railway Village supply, was generally suspect. In 1856 a 'Swindon Water Company' was discussed and an 'ideas' meeting was held in 1857. It was suggested that a survey of the supply should be made and future sources investigated. The survey reported that 'pure water could be obtained from the range of chalk hills lying to the south, and in the immediate proximity of Old Swindon'. It also reported that 'the Wroughton Spring water ran 27 feet under the Goddard Arms Hotel'. Despite the formation of the Swindon Water Company the supply did not improve, and in February 1866 the Company reported:

> 'The water supply for the towns of Old and New Swindon has been for some time insufficient to meet the rapidly increasing wants and requirements of the inhabitants. Old Swindon's supply is derived partly from a stratum of lime and sand rock, partly through wells which in many instances are polluted with sewage and other animal matter, and partly from a spring in the Wroughton Road, where it is fetched in buckets and water carts. The spring is polluted by garbage thrown in by the local inhabitants.
> Water for New Swindon is partly derived from a canal which receives the contents of many house drains, and also from the Wroughton Spring.'

The G.W.R. Company has been drilling deep wells for water in the Westcott Place area, in order to supply the Works, but the attempt failed. Water was found, but not in sufficient quantities. This led to the G.W.R. co-operating with the Water Company, and nominating representatives on the Board. This brought a rapid improvement, and the laying of piped supplies increased throughout the town.

By 1880, the 'Waterworks Company', as it was renamed, was supplying 200,000 gallons per day to Old and New Swindon. A writer of the day claimed,[4] with a lack of diffidence that characterised many Victorian statements, that

> 'filtrated and softened by the famous Porter-Clark system, installed at great expense, the supply is of a degree of perfection hardly to be found in any other town in the country'.

He added that 'water is provided free for the extinction of fires.' He did not mention that the water supply was turned off at 8 p.m. every night; an act that caused a considerable amount of consternation at the meetings of the Local Boards, because, as was sagely pointed out, if a fire occurred after 8 p.m. 'considerable damage would be done to property before a message could be sent to Wroughton for the supply to be turned on.'[5] The Boards decided to make a joint approach to the Postmaster General to ask 'if telegraphic communication by single wire could be made with Wroughton Works'. After a delay of three months the Postmaster General agreed for this to be done at a cost of £43.10.0.[6] One feels sorry for the unfortunate person whose premises caught fire after 8 p.m. during this waiting period.

Street lighting had been installed in the Railway Village by the G.W.R. Company as part of their general plan; the gas being provided by the Company's own Gas Works. The rest of New Swindon was poorly lit, 'during the Winter's nights being left in total darkness'. Old Swindon had a small Gas and Coke Company, (established in 1841), but only provided lighting to private subscribers. In October 1862 an open meeting was held, to discuss the formation of a Swindon Gas Company to provide lighting for the whole of New and Old Swindon. The New Swindon representatives were not enthusiastic and the proposal was turned down. This brought a bitter protest from the leader writer of the 'Advertiser'.[7]

'That mile between the towns is to be continued to stay in darkness - to be continued a spot fruitful in broken shins, concussions and impromptu embraces - a spot where the cadger, garroter and pick pocket may carry on their business with comparative impunity'.

He also compared the public services of New Town with those of Old Town:

'That portion of the Town which belongs to the Railway Company is well lighted and drained, and has an abundant water supply; whilst that portion which does not belong to the Company is very imperfectly drained, has no public lights, and is without a water supply'.

However, a Swindon Gas Company was formed in 1863, and a Gas Works built at Queen Street in 1864. This led to a rapid improvement in the supply, and the pressure of the developing town soon ensured that lighting was provided as the streets were laid down and built up.

As the New Town grew, and the mile long gap between the two towns began to narrow and finally disappear, the call grew for amalgamation, and the creation of a Borough of Swindon. Since the earliest days the G.W.R. Company had administered the Railway Village, and, in effect, New Swindon. There had been very little co-operation between New and Old Swindon in the matter of a general policy of local government for the two districts. In 1864 'Local Boards' - elected bodies responsible for Local administration - had been formed for Old and New Swindon. The Old Town Board members were mainly business men and traders, although the Vicar of Swindon, the Reverend H.G. Baily, and William Morris, the Editor of the 'Swindon Advertiser' both served on the Board for many years. The New Town Board was dominated by representatives of the Railway Company. In the early days the New Town Board met at the Mechanics Institute, and later, in one of the offices in the Works.

Circumstances forced both Boards to act together on certain issues. In 1871 they agreed on the need for an isolation hospital to serve both areas, and in 1877, following a public meeting, agreed to form a School Board to administer the schools of the town, and to shape a common policy for the education of the children of Old and New Swindon.

In the late 1880's the issue of amalgamation was continued in the local press and in the town, and exploratory talks on the subject took place at joint meetings of the Boards. These were not successful; the two Boards had gone their separate ways for so long that a mutual suspicion had grown, and neither Board seemed very willing to lose its identity. In 1894 the Wiltshire County Council made an abortive attempt to gain their agreement on the issue, and two approaches from the New Swindon Board were turned down in 1895 and 1896 by the Old Town Board.

However, public opinion became so strong in favour of amalgamation that the Old Town Board was forced to become more co-operative, and to agree to a meeting with the New Swindon Board to discuss the issue. As a result of this meeting between the Boards, or Councils, as they were by then called, a report was published in March 1897, recommending that incorporation should take place, and the the two towns should be formed into a single rateable area, divided into 6 wards with 6 councillors each. On 23rd November 1897, a public meeting, attended by over 1,000 people, decided, by a large majority, to petition the Privy Council for a Charter of Incorporation which would join the two towns and create the Borough of Swindon. A Privy Council inquiry was held in August 1898, and with no real opposition raised, the Charter was granted, and was received in Swindon on 22nd January 1900, to take effect from the following 9th November.

On that date, sixty years after the arrival of the Great Western Railway, New Swindon and Old Swindon finally merged and became the Borough of Swindon. Predictably, the first Mayor was a railwayman - G.J. Churchward, Manager of the G.W.R. Swindon Works.

place at joint meetings of the Boards. These were not successful; the two Boards had gone their separate ways for so long that a mutual suspicion had grown, and neither Board seemed very willing to lose its identity. In 1894 the Wiltshire County Council made an abortive attempt to gain their agreement on the issue, and two approaches from the New Swindon Board were turned down in 1895 and 1896 by the Old Town Board.

However, public opinion became so strong in favour of amalgamation that the Old Town Board was forced to become more co-operative, and to agree to a meeting with the New Swindon Board to discuss the issue. As a result of this meeting between the Boards, or Councils, as they were then called, a report was published in March 1897, recommending that incorporation should take place, and the the two towns should be formed into a single rateable area, divided into 6 wards with 6 councillors each. On 23rd November 1897, a public meeting, attended by over 1,000 people, decided, by a large majority, to petition the Privy Council for a Charter of Incorporation which would join the two towns and create the Borough of Swindon. A Privy Council Inquiry was held in August 1898, and with no real opposition raised, the Charter was granted, and was received in Swindon on 22nd January 1900, to take effect from the following 9th November.

On that date, sixty years after the arrival of the Grand Western Railway, New Swindon and Old Swindon finally merged and became the Borough of Swindon. Predictably, the first Mayor was a railwayman - C.A. Wheatwind, manager of the G.W.R. Swindon Works.

Notes and references

1. Swindon Advertiser 15th September 1856

2. Ibid. 13th October 1856

3. Ibid. 17th April 1865

4. Astill's Swindon Directory 1880

5. New Swindon Local Board Minute Book 4th March 1880

6. Old Swindon Local Board Minute Book 1st July 1880

7. Swindon Advertiser 4th May 1863

CHAPTER 5

THE RAILWAY VILLAGE AND THE G.W.R. WORKS

By 1860 the Railway Village was complete, and no further extensions or alterations to the layout took place.

This unique settlement, built, almost literally, in the shadow of the G.W.R. Works, was a self contained unit. Its inhabitants could see and hear the broad gauge expresses thundering along the main line, little more than a stone's throw from their cottages. They were completely identified with the Company, insomuch that they worked long hours in the Works and in return were provided with the necessities of life. The Company paid their wages, lit the streets, provided the water supply, educated their children and gave them recreational facilities.

It also exercised a somewhat stern and paternalistic control over its employees, and sanctions were often threatened in reply to alleged misdemeanours by the staff.

In 1856, Mr. I.S. Fraser, the Acting Works Manager, was concerned about the great waste of water in the Village from various causes, but especially from the "Taps being left open". He had a simple remedy for this state of affairs, notice being given 'that if this be continued the water will only be turned on for one hour each day.'[1]

On the death of Mynard C. Rea, in 1857, Mr. William F. Gooch, a brother of Daniel Gooch, became Works Manager and issued an edict against snowballing. It, too, was brief and to the point: 'Any person detected throwing snowballs into or about the entrance of the Works, or within the entrance of the Works will be discharged.'[2] Mr. Gooch seems to have had quite a few staff problems during his tenure of office as manager of Swindon Works, and apparently sabotage was not unknown. In January 1859 he issued a notice that read:

£2 REWARD

'Whereas some evil disposed person or persons put a

piece of gas pipe into the Exhaust part of the Prometheus
Engine between Thursday and Saturday the 20th and 2nd inst.
the above reward will be given to any person who will give
such information as will lead to the conviction of the
offender or offenders.'[3]

However, his main preoccupation seems to have been with the children
of the Railway Village, and in November 1859 he issued a statement full
of veiled threats:

NOTICE

'It having come to my knowledge that many of the boys of
New Swindon are very unruly and mischiev ous in their
conduct, especially during the evening when property is
frequently damaged and, (as on a recent occasion) life
endangered, I hereby give notice that any person in the
service of the Company reported to me as being disorderly,
firing Cannon, or making an improper use of Firearms in
the Village be discharged, and as the Parents in most cases
are to blame for not checking such bad conduct amongst
their children, I consider it my duty for the protection
of the Inhabitants and the Company's property to hold the
Workmen in the Factory responsible for the behaviour of
their children, and shall not hesitate to discharge any
man who allows any of his family to commit such offences.'[4]

What the workmen and their children were doing 'firing Cannon' or
'discharging Firearms' one can only conjecture, but possibly Mr. Gooch
forgot that Guy Fawkes Night is on November 5th. The Railway Village
seems to have been quite a lively place, and one finds Gooch calling
the attention of the Workmen to yesterday's disgraceful and riotous
proceedings in the Works and Village, leading in one case to destruc-
tion of property.' He requests,

'all men who value the peace, good order and respectability
of the Village to use every endeavour to preserve the same
and ensure protection of their neighbours, and report to
me the names of any - and more particularly the leaders -
taking part in such proceedings.'[5]

Gradually, however, the 'Dodge City' atmosphere of the Village seems
to have cooled, and although the reputation of the early navvies who
built the railway and the Works clung to the G.W.R.'s permanent employees
for some time, by the 1870's there was little drunkenness, immorality or
violent crime, and Richard Jefferies comments on the superior intelli-
gence of the workers, stating 'where one book is read in agricultural
districts, fifty are read in the vicinity of the factory.'[6]

Wages in the factory were high compared with those of the predominantly agricultural workers of the rest of the County, and with the ever increasing expansion of the G.W.R. Works, employment was reasonably secure. The Railway Age had moved at express speed all over Britain, and as the network of lines grew and the Great Western Railway system spread, so more and more railway engineering work was required, and most of it found its way to Swindon. One addition, built in 1861, was the Rail Mill, which at full capacity was reckoned capable of producing 19,300 tons of rails a year.[7]

An Almanack for 1864[8] gives an interesting insight into some of the personalities of the Railway Village. An intriguing advertisement is that of 'Miss M. Thomson, Milliner and Dress Maker, 42 Taunton Street, Orders promptly attended to. Pinking neatly done.' Joseph Smith of High Street, proudly proclaims that he sells 'Produce of the Highest Quality including Cheddar, Gloster and American cheese.' Mr. Dixon was the landlord of 'The Cricketers Arms', which still stands right in the middle of the Village.

"Mr. G.R. Swinhoe, Surgeon, London Street,' was the Company's doctor and occupied one of the larger houses in the Village.

The Mechanics Institute is described in detail in the Almanack and one reads that

> 'founded in 1843, it now numbers upwards of 600 members. The noble building of the Institution was opened in 1855. The library contains upwards of 3570 volumes comprising a large number of standard works of fiction, and many valuable works on Science, History, Biography etc. Books are issued on the evenings of Monday, Wednesday and Friday to Members residing at Swindon and on Tuesdays and Thursdays to non-residents. The Reading Room, open every day with the exception of Saturdays and Sundays from 10 a.m. until 1 p.m. and every evening with the foregoing exceptions, from 7 until 10 p.m. and on Saturdays from 4 p.m. until 9 p.m. is well supplied with daily and weekly newspapers, journals and periodicals etc. The Chess and Draughts Room is furnished with all the requisites for the players of those games. A series of attractive Lectures, Musical Entertainments, Dramatic Performances etc., for the season 1863 - 64 will take place. Season

tickets (admitting to the whole of the Entertainments etc.) have been issued by the Council.'

The G.W.R. Medical Fund also widened its activities. In November 1860 the Medical Fund provided Turkish baths, and by 1869, in addition to full bathing facilities, the Fund provided for its members an air-bed and mattress, scales, weights and measures, and the inevitable lime for cleaning, and subscribed to two hospitals in London, two (including an Eye Dispensary) at Bristol, and one at Bath.

What was life like for the worker who lived in the Railway Village during the middle years from 1850-1880? Was it a pleasant well ordered existence where the well paid artisan could watch the cricket in the Park, borrow his books from the Mechanics Institute, take a pint from Dixon at "The Cricketers" and return to his little cottage in Exeter Street, in order to be cheerily on his way to work in the great factory at 6 a.m. the next morning? And could his wife, whilst he was at work, send her children to the G.W.R. school in New Swindon, and take her garments for 'pinking neatly to be done' by dear Miss Thomson at 42 Taunton Street? And then perhaps leisurely purchase her groceries at Joseph Smith's in the Village High Street?

The evidence, however, suggests that life in the Railway Village was not quite so pleasant, certainly not in the early middle years. In September 1853 an outbreak of typhus fever occurred in the Village,[10] and there was a rough element living in the overcrowded cottages. Shops were few in the Village and New Swindon, although the 1851 census shows that there were some dozen inns and beerhouses in the area. A daily market in the High Street commenced in 1854, but the Old Town remained the chief shopping centre for some years, and a weekly shopping parade took the inhabitants of New Swindon up 'a steep and narrow footpath, across stiles and through fields and allotments, from the end of Regent Street to the Castle Inn in Prospect.'[11]

As the years passed the Works expanded steadily, and new businesses continued to open in the New Town. The Railway Village ceased to be a settlement in a rural landscape. By 1880 New Swindon outnumbered the Old Town in the number of its trades people.[12] A sense of community undoubtedly existed amongst the railway workers. They were organizers

SWINDON RAILWAY VILLAGE

The Main Tunnel Entrance of Swindon Works

in London Street

Western Half of Railway Village

Swindon Railway Museum;

formerly the "Barracks" lodging house,

built c.1850

Market Hall, Emlyn Square, c. 1890

Last broad gauge train from Swindon. May 1892
Engine 'Great Western'.

Broad gauge locomotives at Swindon May 1892
for conversion. St. Mark's and Water Tower
in background.

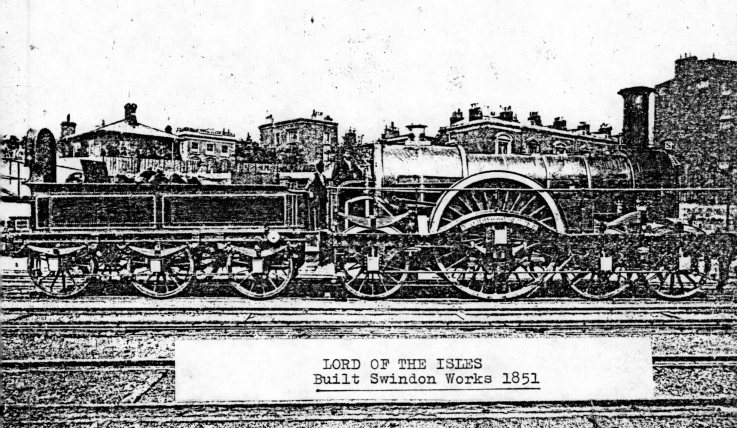

LORD OF THE ISLES
Built Swindon Works 1851

DINING HALL
Swindon Works 1880

Passenger Engine No. 55 'QUEEN'
Designed by Joseph Armstrong, built at Swindon 1873
This engine was used for hauling the Royal Train.
2 - 2 - 2   Driving wheels 7'1½" Withdrawn 1905

(generally with the backing of the Railway Company), of activities such as musical evenings, lectures on foreign countries, firework displays, outings to Oxford and the annual 'Trip' holiday; activities that would be smiled at by modern youth. Living in the Railway Village was always referred to as living in the 'Company's houses'.

Life in the Railway Village seems to have improved in the seventies and eighties, and to have avoided the poverty and worst abuses of the Industrial Revolution. There was plenty of work, a fair wage by the standards of the day, some leisure activities and a sense of belonging. There was, however, one constant fear that lay over the family life of the Village. The infectious diseases of the time, such as scarlet fever, diptheria and others were common, and hard to control by the medical knowledge then available, with the result that the children of the Village were always in danger. Even as late as 1880 the figures of child mortality in the parish of St. Mark's were horrifying.[13] In that year there were 178 funerals at the church, and of these 147 were for babies and children - an average of nearly three a week. In November alone there were 15 funerals, of which 10 were for children eight years of age and under. The grief and sadness caused by such melancholy figures must have been great indeed.

Mention has been made of working conditions in the G.W.R. Works during the earlier years of its existence, and also of its continual expansion. This expansion was not only due to the growth of the Great Western Railway system, but also to the policy of the Directors of the Company in concentrating the whole of the work of building and repairing the rolling stock at one Works. In this they adopted a different attitude from the Boards of other railway companies who preferred to have a separate Works for each main activity. For example, the L.N.W.R. had its main Locomotive Works at Crewe, whilst the carriages were made at Wolverton, and the wagons at Earlestown. The N.E. Railway's Locomotive Works was at Gateshead, and the Carriage and Wagon Works at York. Swindon was not only the Locomotive and Carriage and Wagon works, it was also the Stores Department headquarters, and all these activities were concentrated under one management.

This policy of centralization resulted in the building, in 1868, of the Carriage and Wagon Works, and in a massive increase in the numbers of men employed at Swindon Works. The diversity of the skills of the artisans became remarkable. Coach bodymakers, millwrights, coach trimmers, wagon builders, fitters, boilermakers, painters and many others of strange and specialized skills joined the huge crowds that daily filled the Works entrances. Hundreds of labourers were needed, not only to help the tradesmen in their tasks, but also to clean and maintain the great workshops, and to fetch and carry the materials necessary for the manufacture and repair of the locomotives, carriages and wagons.

Large quantities of castings were made for the Permanent Way and Signal Departments, and a considerable staff was occupied in the construction and repair of Station furniture and fittings. The heavy repairs to the pumping machinery in use at the Severn Tunnel, and the hydraulic machinery at the various Docks and Stations were carried out at Swindon. New foundries were built in 1873 and considerable additions made to the Locomotive Works.[14] As the fleet of Carriages and Vans increased so new workshops were built for their repair, north of the main line.

At the time of the change of gauge in May 1892, the whole of the broad gauge rolling stock was brought to Swindon to be converted or broken up. Thirteen miles of additional sidings were laid to receive this stock. The total number of broad gauge locomotives was 195; of these, 130 had been so constructed that they were readily convertible to narrow gauge. There were also 748 passenger train vehicles, and upwards of 3400 wagons and vans, a large proportion of which had been constructed with a view to conversion. This was especially the case with a number of the eight wheeled carriages which required only the changing of the bogies and the alteration of the footboards to transform them from broad to narrow gauge. On one occasion 25 coaches were so converted in $6\frac{1}{4}$ hours by means of specially constructed hydraulic trap lifts.[15]

In 1892 it was claimed[16] for Swindon Works that "it was the largest establishment in the world for the manufacture and repair of railway engines, carriages and wagons, about 10,000 men being employed under one management."

This huge Works was said to produce 1 new engine per week, 1
carriage per day and 1 new wagon every working hour.[17] The
distribution of staff in 1892 was as follows:-[18]

Locomotive Department	Loco Factory	5000	
	Rolling Mills	300	
	Running Shed	300	5600
Carriage Department	Carriage Works	1800	
	Saw Mill	400	2200
	Wagon Works		1600
	Office Staff		300
	Stores, Platelayers etc.		350
			10,050

By March 1898 the total number employed had risen to 12198.[19]
The Locomotive Works was the showpiece of the complex, mainly
because the repair and building of locomotives was heavy engineering, involving many processes, all of a spectacular nature to the
layman. The Iron Foundry, where iron castings of all descriptions
were produced was particularly impressive, with its huge cupola
furnaces for melting pig iron and scrap. The rail chairs - the
castings which were bolted to the sleepers to support and hold
the rails in place - were manufactured in the Chair Foundry, and
the weekly output of these castings was 9000. Non-ferrous
castings were made in the Brass Foundry, whilst the huge Boiler
Shop was a cacophony of noise as the sheets of metal forming the
engine boilers were rivetted together. By 1892, the Rail Mill,
which had originally been planned to roll out the iron rails for
the track, had changed its function. It became known as the
Rolling Mills, (as did one of the New Swindon public houses), and
was used for rolling bar iron and scrap wrought iron, and had an
average turn out of between 160-200 tons weekly.

The Machine Shop, or R shop, as it was called (all the shops
were lettered), was the pride of the Swindon Works. Here the
turning, shaping, cutting, drilling, planing and milling machines
formed the metal for every part of the locomotive.

The Erecting Shop was a vast workshop where engines of all types were repaired, and where new engines began to take shape in the course of a few days. In addition to the main shops there were smaller ones where the wheel turners, millwrights, patternmakers, toolmakers, coppersmiths and other tradesmen worked.

The whole immense works was under the domination of the Steam Locomotive - that strange invention which had, within the lives of many of the workmen - revolutionised the English scene, not only by its physical presence as it puffed and clattered through the countryside - although, that indeed, was a remarkable enough sight - but also by the ease and speed with which it could move prodigious loads of goods and transport large numbers of people.

As the locomotives, in their various stages of repair or construction, moved through the Works, they were served by hundreds of workmen, each of whom contributed his particular skill or labour. The work was unending; as one engine left the great Locomotive Works ready for service another one arrived to take its place.

The Carriage Works, although not so spectacular as the Locomotive Works, was a large Works in its own right and its role of building and repairing the G.W.R. coaches made the provision of a saw mill necessary, equipped with every type of saw and with mortising and tenoning machines and machines that could plane four sides of boards at one operation. In the Carriage Building Shop every type of coach was built, from the ordinary passenger coach to horse boxes, Post Office vans and saloons. The Trimming and Upholstery Shop, and the Paint and Finishing Shops also played their part in turning out the famous G.W.R. rolling stock.

To the north of the main line was the Wagon Works, which employed hundreds of men in the building and repair of the many types of wagon. In addition there were ancillary services such as stores distribution and platelaying, and hundreds of office and station staff. And still the Works continued to grow!

Notes and references

1. Notice dated 27th November 1856 from "Notices to Foremen and Workmen from the Manager, Swindon Works 1853-1880" (Original Notice Book)

2. Ibid. 3rd February 1858.

3. Ibid. 24th January 1859.

4. Ibid. 10th November 1859.

5. Ibid. 5th February 1859.

6. R. Jefferies. The Hills and the Vales. (London 1882)

7. V.C.H. IX p. 129

8. Dores Swindon Almanack and Public Register (1864) (Swindon Public Library)

9. Swindon Studies p. 116

10. Ibid. p. 100

11. Large. A Swindon retrospect p. 22

12. Kelly's Directory of Wilts. 1880

13. St. Marks Parish magazine. Swindon September 1971

14. Information obtained from a pamphlet "Swindon Works" issued by the G.W.R. Company in March 1898.

15. Ibid.

16. The Great Western Railway's Swindon Works 1892 Published in "Wiltshire Pamphlets No. 27" (Swindon Public Library)

17. Ibid.

18. Ibid.

19. "Swindon Works" March 1898.

CHAPTER 6

PEOPLE AND EVENTS 1854-1901

1854 was the year of the Crimean War. The historic battles of Alma
and Inkerman, Balaclava and Sevastopol loomed ahead, and the Light
Brigade was soon to make its famous Charge at the Russian Guns.
However, to the Reverend Mr. Campbell, Vicar of St. Marks, New Swindon,
there were more pressing matters nearer home - such as the violent
behaviour of his parishioners. On 17th May, the new local paper, the
"Swindon Advertiser and Monthly Record", reported that:

> 'The Rev. Mr. Campbell made a representation to the
> magistrates as to the state of New Swindon. From
> 3 o'clock to 8 on Easter Monday, men were fighting
> opposite the Greyhound Inn in Westcott Place, and
> nothing done about it. P.C.'s Titchener and
> Running said they met in the New Town between 3
> and 4 and then all was quiet. Mr. Superintendent
> Haynes heard there was fighting at New Town, but
> all was quiet when he got there. The magistrates
> thought it was a subject for the Chief Constable's
> interference, and directed Mr. Haynes to make known
> the representation of Mr. Campbell, with a view to
> having a policeman stationed at New Town'.

Such affrays and disturbances were not unusual in 1854 Swindon.
Public Houses such as "The Greyhound" were the centres of social
life for many of the men of the town. The houses in which they
lived were so overcrowded, and the available leisure activities so
limited, that the rough and ready conviviality of the beerhouses
and inns of New Swindon made a great appeal. Most of the men had
no association with the predominantly agricultural background of
Swindon, and the census records show that they came from many
different areas of the country. Fitters from Glasgow and mechanics
from Newcastle mixed with Irish labourers and former Wiltshire farm-
hands; their only common ground being their employment in the
Locomotive Works. They were mostly young men - the records show
that few were over the age of 50 - and young men with enough drive

and spirit to leave their homes, in some cases far distant, and join the 'Railway' - that marvellous undertaking that was revolutionising Victorian Britain. With such a lively mixture of men, and the general 'boom town' atmosphere that prevailed, it was small wonder that violence was never very far from the surface and often erupted.

The violence of New Swindon was complemented by low life in some parts of Old Town, where a few of the public houses were 'dens of iniquity', frequented by prostitutes, rogues and drunks, and open most of the day and night. The "King of Prussia" Inn in High Street with its notorious landlord "Fat Billy Webb", and the "Rhinoceros" Inn in Albert Street, were frequently in the news, and one drunken free for all at the "Rhinoceros" which was described in the 'Advertiser' as 'ending in a violent assault by Charlotte, a young woman of easy virtue, on the land-lord's wife, amid a general uproar', must have been worthy of portrayal by a Cruikshank or Doré. The 'Advertiser's' columns were full of reports of metal thieves, wife beaters, robbers, drunks and attempted suicides. The Police Force of the town consisted of a Superintendent, an Inspector, and two Constables in Old Swindon, and later, (as a result of the Rev. Mr. Campbell's complaint), a Sergeant in New Swindon. They appear to have been fully employed.

Possibly as a counter reaction to this seamy side of life in the town, some of the religious groups adopted a very strict code of conduct for their members, and the minute book of the Newport Street Congregationalists gives details of expulsions of some of the brethren for unseemly behaviour such as 'being seen dancing'.

An important event in New Swindon was the laying of the Foundation Stone of the new Mechanics Institute on 24th May 1854. This was carried out by Lord Methuen, 'with full Masonic rites, and in the presence of thousands of spectators'.

The building was sponsored by the New Swindon Improvement Society, a company formed the previous year with the aim of increasing the leisure and recreational facilities for the people of New Swindon. Concerts, musical evenings, lectures etc. had regularly been held inside the Works, but a new building outside, with facilities for a Market included, was obviously more desirable. The G.W.R. authorities thought so, and provided a site, in the middle of the Railway Village, on a perpetually renewable lease at a nominal rent of 5/- a year. They also gave an annual subscription of £100 a year to the Society's funds. The new building would comprise:

> 'On the ground floor, in addition to the usual offices, hot and cold water baths, a reading room, library, coffee room, council room, housekeeper's room etc. On the top floor a concert hall and stage. At the south end it is intended to erect a series of small shops, which will be let to persons for the sale of various articles required by the inhabitants.'

The event seems to have caused a great deal of excitement and a report tells of the huge crowds present:

> 'From an early hour in the morning great numbers of people arrived from all parts of the country, each succeeding train making great additions to the number already assembled, so that by the commencement of the ceremony of laying the stone, there could not have been less than ten thousand people present.'

After the ceremony there was a 'banquet for 1,000 ladies and gentle-men'. There were also 15 toasts and a 'very merry atmosphere'. The tradesmen of Old Town closed their shops in honour of the distinguished visitors and of the importance of the ceremony. Possibly the fact that many of them were invited to the banquet might have had something to do with their gesture.

The pages of the 'Swindon Advertiser' were filled with the advertisements of the local traders, and amongst those of Blackford the butcher, Saunders the tailor, Reed the fishmonger and Holmes the greengrocer, was one from R. Taylor the chemist, of 1 High Street, New Swindon with his 'Taylor's compound and Rhubarb mixture for Cholera'. One advertisement was in verse and appeared regularly for several years. It told of 'S. Filtness of the Birmingham, Sheffield, London and Staffordshire Warehouse, 40 Newport Street:

> 'Where all may be furnished with goods of the best
> Of the various articles herein expressed.
> Namely, brushes of all sorts, for wet and dry rubbing
> Soft brushes for toilets and hard ones for scrubbing,
> Paint brushes, tooth brushes, hearth brushes and brooms
> With mops of the best yarn for the scrubbing of rooms.

Shoe brushes, horse brushes, curry combs and tin tacks,
Note paper, envelopes and good sealing wax.
Smelling bottles, pins for the hair, and bed sacking;
Bread trays, tea trays, glue and fine japan blacking,
Looking glasses, skimmers, cedar pencils, round and square
And all sorts of china, glass and crockery ware.
Scuttles for coal, or cinders, or ashes,
Hair powder, chalk lines and pulleys for sashes.
Great choice of nick-nacks, combs, ivory and bone.
The very best mouse traps that ever were known.
Pins papered and loose, hooks and eyes and carpenter's flaskets,
American clocks, nut meg graters, and fancy baskets.
Fine razors and knives, and razor strops neat,
Pens, Penholders and shaving boxes complete.
Warming pans, handles and handles for mops
Hand bowls, copper kettles and watering pots;
American tubs, fenders, frying pans, and pails,
Coffin furniture, lace, white and black nails.
Rummers, tumblers and cruets for mustard,
Glass cups, china cups, and cups for a custard.
Saws, chisels, brad awls and hatchets,
Scissors, paper knives, and black lead in packets,
Cotton purses, silk purses and purses of leather,
Umbrellas to keep out the tempestuous weather,
Braces, belts and fancy studs for shirts,
French clogs, plain clogs and pattens to keep from the dirt,
Tin cups and tin kettles and coffee cans,
Boilers, saucepans, door mats and dripping pans;
Tea caddies, work boxes and cinder riddles,
Writing desks, jews harps, whistles and fiddles.
Table knives, carving knives, of the very best steel,
Tapes, ball cotton and cotton on reels.
Shoemakers knives, rasps, an assortment of rules,
Italian irons, flat irons and carpenters tools.
Pictures in gilt and plain frame
And many other articles too numerous to name.
To enumerate all thats sold by this general trader
Would exhaust the patience of writer and reader.'

Supermarkets are supposedly modern creations but Mr. Filtness seems
to have had one in 1854 which in the range and diversity of its stock
cannot be equalled anywhere in the town today. Mrs. O'Connor, also
believed in carrying large stocks at her Boot and Shoe Shop in High
Street. She advertised that there were over 3,000 pairs of shoes for
sale there.

The G.W.R. Company, and especially Swindon Works, was always referred
to with great respect by the speakers and writers of the day. Even an
incident involving a runaway engine was played down, and the following

report was half way down a side column of 'The Swindon Advertiser' of
23rd June, 1854:

> 'On Saturday last one of the passenger train engines
> being left unattended at the Coke Shed, Swindon Station,
> for the purpose of taking in a fresh supply of fuel and
> water, previous to starting on the return journey to
> London, started off at a rapid pace, passing through
> Swindon Station without being in the least alarmed at
> numerous alarming danger signals, or the shouting and
> gesticulations of numerous porters and policemen,
> fortunately, without doing any damage, and proceeded
> on the 'Up' line for a distance of 14 or 15 miles. As
> the engine passed through the station it was fortunately
> noticed by the driver of another engine to be minus
> the driver and stoker: he immediately uncoupled his
> engine, and having got it on the same line of rails
> proceeded after it at full chase, the 'Great Western'
> engine driven by Mr. Appleby, following in the rear.
> Having succeeded in overtaking the engine near Faringdon
> Station, the driver of the second engine succeeded in
> passing from his engine to the runaway one, took charge
> of it and drove it into Faringdon Station, where it was
> shortly afterwards joined to the train it was intended
> to have taken from Swindon, and ultimately arrived in
> London without further mishap.'

What strange combination of mechanical oversights allowed the runaway
engine to commence its unscheduled journey was not stated, but
obviously the brake could not have been applied and the regulator
must have been left open. The whole bizarre incident reads like a
Hollywood thriller of the 1920's, with the three engines careering
along the main line, the shouting porters and gesticulating policemen, the gallant driver overtaking the runaway, his hair raising
climb from one speeding engine to the other, and finally the
screaming brakes as he brings the shuddering locomotive under control.
Across the mists of time he deserves a cheer. What retribution awaited
the employee who berthed the engine at Swindon Coke Shed, and neglected
to make it safe, is another matter. Safety precautions on the line
at Swindon seem to have left considerable room for improvement, for
shortly before the incident of the runaway engine another mishap had
occurred when:

> 'a special train which had been used to convey the
> Duke of Beaufort from Chippenham to Swindon Station
> was returning and came into contact with a brake van
> which had incautiously been left about on the main

line, from a siding opposite Swindon Works. The engine,
which was going at a rapid pace, was greatly damaged by
the collision, also the trucks and carriages'.

No mention was made of the effect the collision had on the engine-
driver and fireman, but at the least, they must have been considerably
shaken. The engine-driver has always been considered to be at the top
of any table of precedence of railway workers. The nature of his duties -
to be in charge of a racing mechanical giant pulling a train of coaches
filled with hundreds of passengers, sometimes in the black of night and
in fair weather or foul - has no similar example of physical or mental
strain in the railway world. Particularly was this so in the early days
of the railways, for the locomotives gave no protection from the elements -
no driver's cab - and the driver and his fireman were often alternately
drenched and then frozen by the effects of the rain and wind. He was
also liable to suffer from incidents and negligence over which he had no
control, such as elementary safety failure which allowed 'a brake van to
be incautiously left about on the main line'. In retrospect, the use of
the word 'incautiously' must have been the understatement of the year 1854.

Another event in 1854 was the death of Ambrose Goddard, the Lord of the
Manor, at the age of 75, following a riding accident. As a young officer
in the 10th Hussars he had fought in the Peninsular War, and had taken
part in Sir John Moore's famous Retreat to Corunna. He was succeeded by
his son, Ambrose Lethbridge Goddard, who for the next 44 years would be
one of the principal figures in the Swindon scene.

A strange little incident, indicative of the place of small children
in early Victorian days, occurred on 18th September, when a local farmer,
Joseph Deacon, brought to court Thomas Richens, a lad 9 years old, and
charged him with 'misconduct in service'. The boy had been employed to
look after sheep and had amused himself by riding on their backs, a
practice which the farmer thought was injurious to the sheep and led to
the appearance of young Richens in the dock. Although he was only 9
years of age, this would not have been considered unusually young for
his employment in agriculture or farming. Indeed, it was the general
opinion of the time that the business of a farm labourer could not be
thoroughly acquired unless work was commenced before the age of 11.

Even so, his arrival at court charged with such an offence was not to the liking of the Swindon magistrates, and Farmer Deacon was told 'to chastise the boy, instead of bringing him before a Court of Justice. The young sheep jockey did not, however, go completely scot free. He was fined 2/6d costs.

The chastising of children also seems to have been a common practice at the Stratton Workhouse, where a great deal of interest was being shown in the case of Houghton, the Workhouse Master, and his drunken assistant, Michael Carey. A Mr. Wheeler, one of the Workhouse guardians, was so incensed with conditions in the Workhouse that he brought a court case against Houghton, accusing him of 'continually beating the Workhouse boys with a large stick and of forcing sixty of them to wash in one tub of water', an ambiguous statement which brings a startling picture to the mind. Carey was in charge of the sick patients, and besides being drunk most of the time, was fond of beating both patients and boys. Houghton denied the charges, and the case was further complicated by the intervention of a Mrs. Faulkner, the Workhouse schoolteacher, who brought her own set of charges against Houghton, one of which was 'introducing the pauper occupants with others of the opposite sex in the pupil teacher's bedroom'. Houghton claimed she had called him 'A lying little fellow, a scamp, a scoundrel and a hopping man'. Why 'a hopping man' was not explained. This unsavoury case, fully reported in 'The Advertiser', dragged on for weeks, and ended with Carey disappearing and Houghton being reprimanded, but still allowed to keep his position as Workhouse Master.

The whole situation bears a strong resemblance to that in which Oliver Twist found himself, with the children being at the mercy of an ignorant tyrant, the only difference being that at Swindon they had a champion in the doughty Mr. Wheeler. School instruction for the Workhouse children was a recent innovation, and 'The Economist' of February 1854, writing of the condition of education in the country, patronisingly declared that 'even the new pauper schools are quite good'.

In May 1855 the Mechanics Institute was opened to the public. In the following years it was to become the social centre of New Swindon, providing musical entertainments, lectures, a library and reading rooms, and a variety of other activities. This strange-looking building (referred to by the speakers and writers of the day as 'the noble building of the Institute'), was also the physical centre of the Railway Village, its Gothic pile towering over the surrounding rows of neat and tidy cottages. The Market adjoining the Institute proved to be a much needed facility, and

> 'The interior on Opening Night presented a gay and
> lively appearance, the company being numerous and
> the show of articles being plentiful and curious,
> ranging from halfpenny herrings and sheeps trotters
> to poultry and ox beef'.

1856 saw the 'Peace and Victory Celebrations' to mark the end of the Crimean War. There were 'displays of fireworks, firing of Cannon and the illumination of the New Swindon Market.' The ordinary Englishman of the time was very patriotic and had no doubts about the superiority of England. The term 'Britain' was infrequently used, but there were many references to 'Old England' and 'John Bull'. In Swindon this patriotism showed itself in various ways, and in Swindon Works 'every man gave one day's pay to help the widows and orphans of soldiers killed in the Crimean War, and some gave two'.

There were celebrations, too, in the Old Town on 22nd December, when Miss Lucy Clarissa Goddard, sister of the Lord of the Manor, married Captain Verschoyle of the Grenadier Guards. The gallant Captain had just returned from fighting the Russians in the Crimea, and hundreds of Swindonians crowded Old Town to see the bride and groom and give them a tremendous send off. Someone who did not feel like celebrating was George Deacon, the Watchmaker and Silversmith, of Wood Street. His premises were broken into, and goods and cash to the value of £600 taken. In those days the loss of such a sum would have meant ruin to many business men, but George seems to have been made of sterner stuff, and by careful management to have got over the loss, and to have built up and passed on a flourishing business that still exists in Wood Street today.

1857 was an election year, and there were many political letters in the 'Advertiser', the editor of which, William Morris, was personally involved in many local issues of the day. He was a Liberal and used his newspaper to express his opinions forcibly, and this often meant using harsh words about opponents of those policies. However, some of his opponents fought back, one writer referring to Morris as 'a viper' and threatening to horsewhip him. On receiving an abusive letter Morris printed it in full, merely adding an editor's footnote saying 'I take no more notice of this than I do the grunting of a pig'. Many of the letter writers used a nom-de-plume and there was an hilarious correspondence over the sacking of the St. Mark's Choir by the Vicar; the chief point at issue being whether it was the choir that could not sing or the church organ that was out of tune.

On a more sombre note, the death of the manager of the Works - Minard C. Rea - at the age of 35, from the all too prevalent tuberculosis shocked the town, and 900 men from the Works followed the cortege to St. Mark's Church.

Parades, processions and celebrations were a feature of life in the town. Given an occasion of sufficient importance or interest, the people, young and old, attended almost en masse. Such an occasion occurred when Queen Victoria's daughter, The Princess Royal, 'Our Darling Vicky', married Frederick, Prince of Prussia, and Swindon celebrated the event. The 'Advertiser' reported:

> 'Tuesday, 26th January 1858 was a day long to be
> remembered in the town of Swindon. It was truly
> a day of rejoicing and gladness. Everything seemed
> to conspire to render the day worthy of the great
> occasion set apart by the inhabitants, to
> celebrate the wedding of England's Pride and
> Prussia's Glory. A triumphal arch was erected
> bearing the Union Jack and the Prussian Eagle
> with the inscription "The Protestant Alliance".
> Before sitting down to eat the 850 diners formed
> up in a procession in the following order.
> The Union Jack (borne by Master New)
> A body of the Wiltshire Constabulary, clearing the way.
> The New Swindon Brass Band
> The Monster Plum Pudding
> (weighing ¾ of a hundred weight and borne on a barrow
> by two men. In the centre was a very beautifully made
> white satin flag, bearing the inscription "Prussia's
> Hope marries England's Pride")
> The Vicar of Swindon (The Rev. H.G. Baily)
> The Holders of the tickets, headed by the Carvers.'

As the procession moved off, to the cheers of the onlookers and to the blare and crash of the marching band, none present could have thought that in sixty years time the 'Protestant Alliance' would be no more, and that Prussian and Englishman would be engaged in the life and death struggle of the Great War of 1914 - 1918. None present could have guessed, also, that by a strange irony of fate, the son of the Royal Couple whose marriage they were celebrating would be a Prince Wilhelm, later to be Kaiser Wilhelm II and Germany's 'War Lord' in that same conflict.

Two or three times a year the Circus came to town. A typical visit was that from 'Cinnets Mammoth Circus' in 1858. A preliminary notice in the local newspaper informed everyone that 'the parade would start from the Wharf, near Cricklade Road, headed by 4 live geese in hand, harnessed to a washing tub'. Following on this bizarre sight was a brass band, bare back riders, clowns, minstrels and 'little piebald ponies'. From Cricklade Road they marched to Old Town and then down to New Swindon, followed by the greater part of the youth of Swindon. They then returned to the "Bell Close", a large field at the back of the "Bell" hotel and pitched their tent for the performance. One hopes that after that effort the marching geese were excused duty for the rest of the day.

In the outside world the Relief of Lucknow brought the Indian Mutiny to a close and added half a continent to the control of the British Crown, but in Swindon there was a matter of more immediate concern. Why should the price of bread be 9d a gallon in New Swindon and 10d a gallon in Old Swindon? Bakers, shopkeepers and the public joined in a furious debate which continued for some weeks. There seemed to be no sound reason why there should be a different charge except, perhaps, as one correspondent claimed - 'the people in New Swindon won't pay more than 9d a gallon or 2¼d for a 2lb loaf, but the bakers think they can get away with a penny extra charge in Old Town'.

In 1859 Swindon Cricket Club moved to a new ground at the Okus Fields in The Sands. Previously they had played at The Butts, a field adjoining the present Croft ground. Cricket was very popular in Swindon. The Old Swindon side was made up of professional and business men such as the solicitors Bradford, Crowdy and Kinneir, the doctor, John Gay, and tradesmen Tarrant, King, Hawkins and Edmonds. Earlier players included the Budds of Elcombe Hall, both members of the famous 'All England XI'. 'Old' Budd played in a silk top hat and was described as being as 'active as a panther or cat'. In the 1855 side was a certain Nelson, a relation of the famous Lord Nelson, and he was the 'star' player of the team.

New Swindon also had a fine side and had played at The Park since 1847. The standard of play was high and in the ensuing years the two clubs, apart from a fierce rivalry between themselves, also played most of the best club sides in the West of England. In 1856 the G.W.R. side had played at Lords, the headquarters of Cricket, beating the local St. Johns Wood Club. Dr. W.G. Grace played against both sides many times, and not always with great success. In 1869 he did make 111 for Stapleton against the G.W.R. side but a few years later, at the height of his powers, the great 'W.G.' was dismissed for 0 in both innings by Laverick, a New Swindon player, who thus ensured for himself an honoured and never to be forgotten place in the annals of Swindon Cricket.

From the green fields of summer and the sound of bat on ball to ice skating on the frozen Coate Water was a frequent seasonal transition in the town. The hard winters of the time often froze the Wilts and Berks Canal and the Reservoir and in January 1861 it was reported:

> 'For some weeks past Coate Water has been frozen
> over, with ice a foot thick, and the inhabitants
> of the town have sported on its surface on skates
> at hockey, at foot-ball, and such other games as
> their ingenuity devised and the state of the
> weather sanctioned'.

On this occasion someone had the bright idea of holding a barbecue on ice for the poor of the town. A public subscription raised £10, with which it was decided to buy two sheep and roast them on the ice. The Town Crier was told to announce the event in the town, which he seems to have done with good effect, for no less than 1,500 turned up for the free meal. The local land-lords also arrived and set up bars, and as the beer and spirits began to flow, the festivities began to get a little out of hand. The report continued, more in sorrow than in anger:

> 'The sheep were roasted just near enough to the
> lake to say they were on the ice. An Aunt Sally
> had been set up, and a pony was drawing a cart
> over the ice, whilst several were on horseback
> riding on the frozen lake. In the scramble for

> the sheep several children got wet through. The roasting
> left much to be desired, some of the meat being over done,
> some half done, and some not done at all. The last scene
> I saw as I left the festivity was a woman dead drunk being
> wheeled home on a pair of trucks'.

One is struck by the enthusiasm of the people of the town for a special
occasion, and their readiness to join in any activity, whether it was a
cricket match, a procession, a circus or such a festivity as the Coate
Water barbecue. This cannot be wholly explained by the fact that they
had 'to make their own fun'. One senses a feeling that they realised
life could be short, and they were determined to have a part in anything that might be going.

Two cases involving young people illustrate the impermanence of life
in the town in 1862. One was that of poor Barbara Patterson, of New
Swindon, the leading amateur singer of the town.

> 'Miss Barbara Patterson, age 22, through her connections
> with the Swindon Musical Classes, was well known both in
> the town and the neighbourhood. Her amiable manners and
> happy disposition had also secured for her a large circle
> of private friends. It is with sorrow we have to report
> that after complaining of feeling unwell on the Sunday
> afternoon, she died on the Monday night. We understand
> that the cause of death was the bursting of an internal
> abscess, the discharge of which had been so great as to
> flood the heart and stop its free action. At the funeral
> the Free Christian Church was full to overflowing, with
> many hundreds of sad people outside.'

Alas, for poor Barbara, appendicitis operations were not available in
1862.

The other event was the death of a boy called Leech, who had been
killed in an accident in the Works. The Reverend Mr. Campbell came in
for heavy criticism from Morris over the funeral arrangements for the
dead boy. We read:

> 'The fearful death of a lad named Leech occurred in the
> Swindon Railway Works, in consequence of his entanglement
> in the driving straps connecting some powerful machinery.
> This lad, although but 12 years of age, had for some time
> been engaged in the good work of earning his own livelihood
> by honest labour. He was a good lad, and a great favourite
> with the men in the shop in which he worked, and after his
> death the men were anxious to pay to his memory that
> tribute of respect which his winning manners had earned
> for him during his short career among them. A subscription
> was at once started to pay the costs of his funeral. Unfortun-
> ately the poor lad had never been baptised. So was an
> opportunity presented for those who account the Christian
> ceremony of more moment than a Christian life, and being in

> charge of the only burial ground in the district,
> to strut triumphantly on their brief stage and deny
> Christian burial to the body. It was ordered that
> the corpse should be conveyed to its last resting
> place at night, and then placed next to a suicide.
> We have not the space to describe the effect produced
> on many of the mechanics of New Swindon, and not one
> of them will entertain a higher respect for the church
> or its officers.'

Morris coupled with the report a demand for a public cemetery for
Old and New Swindon.

Two more of the strange events which seemed regularly to occur in
the town were the 'stealing of a performing dog, worth £20, from
George Trot, the landlord of the "Lord Raglan" inn, and the
discovery of the remains of a new born child in a loft at the
"Goddards Arms Hotel". The report on this occurrence ended with
a warning - 'There are rumours, and it is better not to allude to
them'. Another celebration, in March 1863, marked the marriage of
the Prince of Wales, the future King Edward VII, to Princess
Alexandra of Denmark. The usual illuminations, fireworks and
procession marked the event, and each child in the town received
a slice of plum cake and two oranges.

The great Railway Works was growing every year, and so was the
traffic at the Station. The arrangement whereby all trains stopped
at Swindon for ten minutes in order that the passengers could take
refreshments, if they so wished, meant that the Station and the
Refreshment Rooms were always busy. The continual arrival and
departure of the passengers, their differences in class, dress and
demeanour, the gruff cries of the porters, the excited chatter of
children, and the intermittent dull rumble of the locomotives
combined to produce an extraordinary medley of sight and sound.

Here could be seen, perhaps, a heavy Victorian father, top hatted
and self assured, pompously directing his wife and family into the
first class room, whilst in the third a workman and his shy young
wife ate meat pies, he with evident enjoyment, but she a little
self consciously and so genteelly.

A description of the Refreshment Rooms in a local directory,
published in 1864, reads, in flowery language:

> 'The magnificent Refreshment Rooms at Swindon Station
> rank amongst the finest in England, and, as every

train stops here for ten minutes, afford excellent
accommodation to the many thousands who daily alight
at this important junction. The Queen and members of
the Royal Family have been entertained here.'

In 1865 President Lincoln was assassinated, and at home the Prime
Minister, Lord Palmerston died. He was a major figure in mid-Victorian
England, and the 'Advertiser' showed its respect by producing a mourning
issue, in which the column divisions were printed with thick black lines.

The new Corn Exchange in Market Square was ready for opening in 1866.
In 1853 a 'Town Hall and Market House' had been erected, but although
this building had been of some service to the town in many ways, such
as that of holding meetings and the transaction of magisterial business,
it was never the least service as a Market House. In 1863 the Swindon
Central Market Company was formed to build a spacious Market House and
Corn Exchange. The new building, 110 feet long and 50 feet wide, with
a 'noble clock tower 80 feet high' was indeed, one of which the town
could be proud, and although there were differences of architecture
between the old 'Town Hall' building and the new Corn Exchange, the
general effect was, and still is, of an outstanding and imposing
edifice.

Such a building deserved a worthy opening, and on 9th April 1866, a
public dinner was held to mark the event. Four of the local landlords,
Westmacott of the "Goddards Arms", Godwin of the "Bell" and his namesake
from the "Kings Arms", together with Washbourne of the "Masons Arms",
were given the task of planning the dinner. All the local dignitaries
were present when Mr. Richard Strange took the chair, and the serious
business of the dinner commenced. After dinner toasts were drunk to the
Queen, Prince of Wales, Bishops and Clergy, Army, Navy, Yeomanry, and
Volunteers, Members of Parliament for North Wilts and Cricklade, Success
to the Swindon Central Market Company, Health of the Chairman, the
Visitors, the Dealers, the Builder, Mr. Phillips, Mr. Read and many
others. For entertainment there was an impromptu rhyming singer, who
sang little couplets about the notabilities present, followed by a
catch phrase 'Says old John Bull'. His efforts were greeted with roars
of laughter and applause and more toasts. By the time the Chairman
proposed the toast of 'The Ladies, the 'Advertiser' reported:

'The uproar in the room was so great that his words
could scarce be heard. The band struck up the
National Anthem as a signal to depart but the
committee informed those remaining that the proceedings had by no means terminated. A new Chairman,

First-class refreshment room in 1852
Swindon Station

Queenstown Bridge over Wilts and Berks Canal 1885

Mr. W. Read was voted in, more toasts were drunk, and the proceedings went on to a very late hour. What happened to the old chairman was not stated, but one can hazard a guess. It seems to have been a night to remember.

In 1867 the Government, under Disraeli, brought in the Electoral Reform Bill. This important measure extended the franchise to include all householders in towns. Before this Bill became law only 4.7% of the population were entitled to vote, and those that were found their initiative and choice were limited by custom, tradition and local interest. The Reform Bill added one million new voters, and doubled the electorate. The effects of the Bill were felt in Swindon, and the election campaign of 1868 was fought with an intensity that had not been experienced in any previous election. The candidates were the Honourable F.W. Cadogan, for the Liberals, and Sir Daniel Gooch and Ambrose Lethbridge Goddard for the Conservatives. There were 2 seats. Morris and the "Advertiser" were solidly behind Cadogan, whilst the "North Wilts Herald" (first published in 1861), and its editor, J.H. Piper, supported the two Conservatives.

With the commencement of the campaign the 'dirty tricks department' of each side was soon in action. Piper pointed out that Cadogan was a stranger to the town - a political carpet-bagger - and made a series of character smears against him. One of them alleged that whilst holding public office he had accepted bribes from a contractor, and another claimed that as Chairman of the Submarine Telegraph Cable Company he had engaged in shady speculation. It was also suggested he was a secret Roman Catholic. Morris, in the "Advertiser", claimed that men in the Works were being given time off, at full pay, to canvass for Sir Daniel Gooch, and that pressure was being put on the men to ensure they voted Conservative. This led, at a chance meeting, to a physical assault on Morris by Joseph Armstrong, the Works Superintendent. Morris, never one to minimise an incident, claimed that Armstrong 'was literally foaming at the mouth', but Armstrong denied the charge. The alleged assault weapon was Armstrong's malacca cane, which Armstrong claimed he 'had merely raised in a reproving manner'.

There were several such incidents in a bitter campaign marked by personal vilification and abuse from both sides. The result of the election was:

Hon. F.W. Cadogan (Liberal)	2844
Sir Daniel Gooch (Conservative)	2452
A.L. Goddard (Conservative)	2009

For several months after, the arguments continued. Cadogan brought an action for libel against Piper, claiming damages of £3,000. Piper fought the case, pleading justification and won a moral victory when Cadogan was awarded a paltry £20 damages, the London "Times" remarking that 'he was ill advised to bring the case to court'.

1868 saw an outbreak of Fenianism throughout the country. This militant movement, which demanded Home Rule for Ireland, caused a scare at Swindon, when Fenian emissaries were reported to be planning bomb attacks on the G.W.R. Works. Special police were enrolled and a day and night watch mounted in the Works, but no attack was made.

A very important step forward for the town was the announcement by the Swindon Water Company that it was now prepared 'to put a water supply into Old Town'. The condition of Old Town, and Newport Street in particular, was, in 1868, deplorable. A letter to the "Advertiser" stated:

> 'Newport Street and its purlieus seeth and reeks with
> pestilence; disease and death are engendered, whilst the
> lists of mortality are swollen to the grief of many and
> the concern of all. 53 people use 3 closets and there
> is no water fit to use. The promiscuous huddling to-
> gether of the sexes in many cases seems unavoidable as
> long as families occupy such dwellings, and must destroy
> all sense of decency, and virtue become but an empty
> name'.

The sewers that had been laid in 1858 were inadequate, and until a piped water supply and water flushed sewers could be provided there was bound to be trouble. Conditions of life in Swindon at the time, although not so bad as existed in many other towns and cities in the country, were, by modern standards, primitive.

Many of the houses were lit by oil lamps, or even candles. The only form of heating was coal or wood, and cooking was done on a range situated in the living room. Very few houses had bathrooms; washing one's face and hands was done in the kitchen sink, and the weekly bath for the children - and sometimes the adults - was taken in a portable iron bath in front of the fire in the living room. Lavatories were outside the house and often shared with another family. Such refinements as toothpaste and special toilet rolls were not used by the ordinary working families. Most of the houses were overcrowded, and 'lodgers' were accepted members of the home. Husband and wife shared their bedroom with the younger children. The workers and any lodgers were up at 5 a.m. in order to get ready for work. Teenage daughters had to help to get the younger children ready for school and help with the other household tasks. Food was rough and ready, with bread and butter or dripping or lard playing a big part in the meals. On Saturday evenings the weekly joint was purchased from the butcher, and the time that the purchase was made was a consideration because prices dropped as closing time approached. The weekly joint would appear in several of the following week's menus. The wives of Swindon's working men of 1868 had the unenviable task of managing the household, providing meals, bearing and looking after the children, doing the washing and other household chores without any labour saving devices. Illness, of which there was plenty, was a disaster, and child mortality was a constant fear. In February 1868 an anonymous poem called "Our first lost" appeared in the "North Wilts Herald", the first verse of which ran:

> 'Two little waxen hands
> Folded soft and silently,
> Two little curtained eyes
> Looking out no more for me.
> Two little snowy cheeks
> Dimpled - dented nevermore,
> Two little trodden shoes
> That will never touch the floor.'

Modern critics would probably dismiss this as mawkish Victorian sentimentality but it might not have appeared so to the Swindon mothers of 1868, many of whom had suffered such a bereavement.

On 1st April 1868 The Swindon Lady Day Fair took place. As usual the townspeople were there to see the fun:

> '... the day being fine the attendance was large; in
> fact, generally speaking, the fair was the largest
> known for many years. The number of servants to be
> hired was perhaps under the average. Good servants
> do not now need to attend a fair or 'mop' to be

hired - and as a consequence the class of servant on
offer - we are obliged to use the term, although it
sounds degrading to speak of human beings as if they
were cattle - was not on the whole, of the highest.
The attendance of showkeepers, itinerant vendors,
gamblers, thieves and vagabonds was unusually large.
During Sunday large numbers of caravans, carts and
other vehicles had assembled on the various roads
leading to the town. They were not allowed to enter
the market place until after the evening service at
places of worship. Between 8 and 9 permission to
enter was given by the police, and a rush was made
for the Market Place, vehicles being driven at a rapid
rate by loud voiced men and women, whose profane
language was disgustingly profuse. Amid curses and
blaspheming the various parties contested their places,
and preparations were made for the morrow. On the day
there were the usual exhibitions, with showily painted
outside illustrations and very tame inside representations.
The public taste today seems to appreciate what may be
termed natural monstrosities. Thus there was a booth
devoted to the exhibition of a man malformed in a manner
which cannot be described, and close by another
exhibition which included a cow with an incredible
number of legs, and a sheep to match. The establishment
was 'touted' over by a female whose earnestness, and
power of rough elocution would have gratified any
public orator, and established a woman's fitness for
public speaking. A boxing booth, the rendezvous of
some half dozen pugilistic rascals; peepshows with
indecent pictures, gaming tables and photographic
establishments helped to make up the whole. We must
not omit to mention a brace of vendors of quack
medicines. There were more thieves present than the
Supt. of Police can remember, and a goodly number were
captured. The "social evil" was largely represented,
the woman old in sin - bloated, repulsive and
calculated to create only disgust in the mind of any
decent man - and the young girl just entering upon
a life of evil, were among those captured by the
police.'

The fairs continued to be held for many years after, although their
original 'servant hiring' purpose ended with the growth of the local
newspapers and their 'Situations Vacant' columns.

Some light relief came in 1868 with the strange case of the Reverend
F.R. Young, a Unitarian minister of strong Conservative views. He had
studied faith Healing during a visit to America, and on his return to
Swindon put his theories to practical test with startling results.
Under the heading 'The New Swindon Miracle Maker', Morris printed a
tongue in cheek account in the "Advertiser" of the Reverend's first
'miracle':

'A Mrs. Joseph Jones of 7 Alma Terrace, was struck
with paralysis and lost the use of her lower limbs.
She could not dress without assistance. She was
visited by the Reverend F.R. Young, the Unitarian
Minister, who asked if he might treat her. In the
presence of another woman he first stroked her
legs from the legs downward several times, praying
earnestly. He then made a mesmeric pass in front
of her face and commanded her to get up and walk.
The poor woman - we have these facts from her own
mouth - says her feelings at the time were
indescribable. She got up and walked'.

Such a report was bound to bring a series of letters from the nom-de-
plume writers, and 'One who knows' was soon in print with

'The Reverend Young has a paralysed eye. Why can't
he cure that? It is astonishing what excitment will
do, particularly when a gentleman such as the
Reverend Young produces that state by "stroking
down a woman's legg"'.

There were others of the same kind, and one of the Reverend's
friends was moved to write about the 'unmitigated slander and
abuse that has been heaped on Mr. F.R. Young, and the filthy
insinuations with which his character has been aspersed'. The
'New Swindon Miracle Maker' correspondence went on for months.

More important to the town was the decision to build a
Carriage and Wagon Works at Swindon. The centralisation of all
building and repair activities for the G.W.R. at Swindon meant that
thousands of new jobs would eventually be created. The new Works
was built in 1868 and was in production by 1870.

On 14th May 1869, Police Sergeant Stevens had a 'Close Encounter
of the Third Kind'.

'About 2 a.m. on Friday, 14th May, as P.S. Stevens
was standing in Taunton Street, he was startled by
a very brilliant white light overhead. On looking
up he saw a large globe of perfectly white fire
descending towards him. When it came within about
100 yards of him, it suddenly turned red, throwing
out a number of sparks like a rocket. It
continued red until it came within 30 yards of the
ground, then turned green and quickly disappeared.
The light from the object was so brilliant that
everything around was distinctly seen, and the
sudden change to darkness produced a very
peculiar effect'.

1870 saw the start of the Franco-Prussian War, whilst at home
there was a growing awareness by the working class of the power of
collective action. Disraeli's Trade Union Act of 1871 stated that

collective action by workers was a lawful method of retaining and
raising wages and in Swindon there was a perceptible change in the
attitude of the railway workers. Collective action was taken in
September 1872, when a petition was sent to the directors of the
Company. It read:

'Gentlemen

We, the undersigned employees at Swindon
Works, do most respectfully lay our memorial before
you, soliciting that you would grant to us, owing to
to the very high price of provisions and other
accessories of life, ten per cent to our day wages
and piecework prices.

Your memorialists would also, Gentlemen, most
respectfully ask you, knowing the extra nourishment
required to serve a man working overtime, to grant
time and a quarter for the first two hours, time and
a half for all hours afterwards, Sundays, Christmas
Day and Good Friday to be paid double time as was the
original custom here.

Your memorialists consider it a very great
hardship for a man to be deprived of all the time
allowed for overtime during the week, should he be
necessitate to lose a day through illness or private
business, therefore we ask that each day should stand
upon its own bottom.

By granting this request, we remain,
Gentlemen, your most respectful and
obedient servants,
The Working Men of Swindon Works

The request was 'not entertained' by the Directors, but the time was
coming when such requests would not be so summarily dismissed.

The '9 Hour Movement' was formed to campaign for a shorter working
week, and its supporters were not confined to the railway workers. A
local master plumber had sacked some of the men in his employ for taking
part in the campaign, and in return received another and less polite
memorial:

'Spreadbury

As I was going up the street today I herd
ever so many men talking about your Damd mean trick
you served your men by giving them a weeks notice
because they stuck up for their rights the 9 hr
movement and they likewise said they would wait on
you some night and see what they can do for you and
I dont blame them either

I am, sir,
The Undertaker
Insure yourself
they said they will have it   '

Mr. Spreadbury said this threat didn't worry him, but gave so many excuses for his dismissal of the men, that it was evident that he was far from happy about 'The Undertaker's' little note.

A peaceful example of the value of collective action was the progress made by the New Swindon Industrial Co-operative Society. Started in 1862, with a few men 'selling a box or two of herrings in a little room at the old "Barracks" building', the movement had gradually grown. A shop was rented in the New Swindon Market, and proved to be such a success that by 1874 the Society was able to build its own premises in East Street.

In the next few years the people were occupied with the opportunities and problems that the accelerating rate of development brought to the town. New businesses, building societies, increasing leisure facilities, trade unions and the ever growing Works left little time for anything else. A General Election was held in 1874, but in Swindon this passed in relative peace, compared with the previous one. This time the Conservatives took both seats with Cadogan coming in a poor third.

There was talk of a new railway - the 'Swindon, Marlborough and Andover' - with a tunnel running through the town, but in 1877 this project was abandoned, and a new route, via Rushey Platt and Okus, chosen in its place.

By 1880 Swindon was a well established and thriving town. The pages of the "Swindon Advertiser" for that year teem with reports of activities of all kinds: club meetings, temperance societies, fur and feather shows, fairs and markets, cricket matches, political meetings and even riots. Everybody seems to have been involved in something, however strange or unusual. It is also strange to see how the passage of time has altered the relative importance of some of the items of news that appeared in the newspaper. The Zulu War had just ended, and a modern reader (especially one who had seen the film "Zulu") would have imagined that the accounts of Isandawala and the epic defence of Rorke's Drift, complete with banner headlines and eyewitness statements, would have filled the columns of the paper. This, however, was not the case. An account there certainly was - a measured appraisal of the campaign, and its implications for Britain's interests in South Africa, some criticism of the administration, and finally a few words of praise for the troops, who had acted with the expected bravery. Given equal prominence was a long account of the Swindon and North Wilts Poultry and Dog Show with the interesting information that 'Mr. G.R. Brett was judge of the cats'.

Throughout the town was felt the power and presence of the great Railway Works. In 1880 work dominated the lives of the people of Swindon to an extent that nowadays is scarcely conceivable. The loss of one's job - at any level - was a major calamity in Victorian England, and security of employment was worth almost anything to the average man. In Swindon the Railway Works provided this security. By 1880 the 'Railway' had increased its hold over the nation. In 1850 British railways carried 67.4 million passengers; in 1875 490.1 million and by 1880 over 500 million. The freight load had more than trebled during the same years. The mileage of track lengthened everywhere, but in addition, the tracks themselves thickened as the swelling demands turned single tracks into double, and double into quadruple. New yards, new sidings and, of particular importance for Swindon, new locomotives, new carriages and new wagons, were constantly required. With such an assured work load the G.W.R. could provide thousands of Swindon workers with steady employment and its massive size enabled it to ride out minor industrial storms. There were side benefits such as the Medical Fund, the Mechanics Institute with its library, the Sick Club and a model village where many of the men lived. These facts were realised and appreciated by the people of Swindon, and criticism of the G.W.R. was rarely heard. It was once said that "what is good for General Motors is good for America", and in 1880 it was generally felt in the town that what was good for the G.W.R. was good for Swindon.

The Locomotive, Carriage and Wagon Superintendent of Swindon Works was William Dean, who had succeeded Joseph Armstrong upon the latter's death in 1877. Under these officers Swindon Works steadily built up a reputation for skilled work and dependable rolling stock, but neither of

them was an engineering innovator of the same class as Sir Daniel
Gooch or George Jackson Churchward.

Factory employment for women was mainly confined to the clothing
company of Comptons, in Sheppard Street, which in 1876 employed
over 300. In 1876 the G.W.R. began to employ women as seamstresses
in the Carriage Works Trimming Shop, but the number was not large.
There was nothing like the large scale employment of women that there
is today, and openings for higher education or training for the
professions simply did not exist.

By 1880 the early and middle Victorian idea that leisure should
be devoted to self improvement, and nothing else, had largely disappeared. Although the Mechanics Institute, with its reading rooms
and public lectures, was still very popular, entertainment of a
different kind was now required by the townspeople. Concerts,
railway excursions, music hall shows and dances became part of the
Swindon leisure scene. Sport began to take an important place in
the life of the town. Cricket had always been popular, and a
Rugby Football club had played against Cirencester College in 1870,
but Association Football now made its appearance, and with the
imminent formation of the Swindon Town Football Club, it soon took
over as the main sporting interest of the town. Soccer seemed to
flourish in an industrial environment, and as the Saturday afternoon holiday spread across the country so were inter town matches
arranged and leagues formed. Locally, teams crystallised around
such groups as Sunday Schools, church and chapel youth clubs,
institutes and industrial concerns, and public houses. Swindon
became, (and has remained), a football town.

There was also a great interest in Horse Racing, and every
shop in the Works had its "bookie's runner", who collected the bets
of the workmen and arranged their delivery to one of the local
bookmakers. Swindon was near to Beckhampton, Lambourn, Foxhill
and other famous racing stables, and betting on racehorses was
wide spread. The "North Wilts Herald" ran a weekly column giving
'form' and 'tips', whilst the "Advertiser" gave wide coverage to
the national meetings.

However, sport and entertainment was not the only leisure occupation of the people. For many of them the main influence was that of Religion. As the churches and chapels were built to meet the spiritual needs of the fast developing town, so an almost evangelical spirit inspired the ministers and their congregations. St. Saviour's (1890), was, for example, built by the voluntary labour of the congregation in their limited spare time. Men and women devoted themselves to church work. There was a great interest in missionary work, and every church and chapel had its young peoples club. The Sunday School movement catered for the children, and every Sunday afternoon hundreds of them, washed and in their 'Sunday Best', made their way to the various church school rooms to hear a Bible Story and be given an illustrated card - a 'Text' - depicting a biblical scene.

In 1880 there was another Parliamentary Election in the town, and the declaration of the poll was the signal for a serious outbreak of rioting. The Liberal candidate, N. Story Maskelyne, headed the poll, and his supporters, or at least a large selection of them, got out of hand, with the result that:

> 'Shortly after the close of the poll an immense crowd
> began to assemble in Bridge Street, and for 2 or 3
> hours the road was impassable; the declared intention
> of some of the crowd being to duck in the canal two
> of the New Swindon publicans who had made themselves
> unusually active in the Conservative interest through-
> out the election. Foiled in this intent, the crowd
> between 7 pm and 8 pm, made for the "Artillery Arms",
> the windows of which they completely smashed. They then
> proceeded to the "Golden Lion Inn" and served it in a
> like manner. The "Volunteer", the "Union", the "Great
> Western Hotel", the "Queens Hotel", the "Locomotive"
> and the "Cricketers' Arms" were next visited. Then
> to Old Town to do the same to the "Kings Arms", the
> "Goddards Arms", and the "Masons Arms". Private
> houses in Prospect Hill shared the same fate. At
> 9 o'clock a large body of police arrived on the
> scene, and although the streets were crowded for
> some time no further trouble took place.'

The statement that 'no further trouble took place' was certainly not the experience of young Mr. A.J. Findlay, of 8 Catherine Street, New Swindon, who in a letter to the "Advertiser" headed "Police Brutality" described his story of the eventful night:

'I wish to register my humble protest against the arbitrary and brutal conduct of the police on the night of the election. I had been in my house the whole of the evening whilst the disorderly mobs were about, but, however, urgent business made it imperative for me to go to the Railway Station. I went there at 11 o'clock, and after transacting my business, was returning to my home. When coming down Bridge Street, I was suddenly stopped by 2 policemen who, without a word, knocked me down with their staffs and brutally beat me over the head and legs. As soon as I could get away from them I ran towards my home and had got as far as the "Locomotive", when another police officer rushed at me and struck me two or three blows with his truncheon, which caused me great pain and terror. At last I arrived home in a pitiable condition, and have suffered severely since from the effects of the zeal of these officers. Are people going about their lawful business to be wantonly attacked and half killed by those who are paid to protect them?

Mr. Findlay apologised most humbly to the Editor for intruding on the space of the paper to recount his melancholy experience. Election Night in Swindon in 1880 seems to have been another night to remember. One wonders, also, as to the nature of the 'urgent business' that young Mr. Findlay had at 11 o'clock at the Railway Station.

On Wednesday 19th January 1881, Swindon experienced the worst snowstorm in the memory of its oldest inhabitants, or of any records in the history of the town. For 12 days prior to the storm, the weather had been brilliant and clear, although bitterly cold, with temperatures of between 10 and 25 degrees of frost. When the storm began the snow fell:

'as no snow had ever been seen to fall before, of such a thickness as to blanket out the light, and of such an amount it seemed as if it would never stop. Soon every street in the town was 3 feet deep in snow, and every house front was snowed up to a height of 5 feet, and 10 feet on the pavements where it had drifted.'

The storm continued for 2 days; there were no newspapers or post, and no connection between London and Swindon. There was great distress in the town. Nor was any help to be obtained from the neighbouring towns, for the extraordinary 'Deep Snow of 1881' was nationwide, and has become a legend in the history of England's weather.

The main Great Western Railway line from Paddington to Bristol was impassable, and gangs of men, hundreds strong, were organized in Swindon Works and put to work in clearing the line. In one case a whole train, complete with passengers, was dug out from its covering of snow.

The great snowstorm indirectly led to an unusually bitter attack on the G.W.R. Company in the "Swindon Advertiser". For some time previously the Company had adopted an uncompromising attitude in all its negotiations with the employees, and this attitude was compared with the efforts of the men in clearing the line. An article from the 'Railway Review' was reprinted, which stated

> 'The work of clearing the line was hard, cold, difficult work for the men called out. A comparison of their conduct, with the conduct of the Company towards them, is worth a passing notice. There happens to be surplus labour in the country, so their rates of wages have been lowered, their hours of duty increased, invidious classification with a view to reducing wages invented and put in force, overtime pay refused, and the treatment of the men made more harsh than before. All this is done that a little more dividend may be shared, and some faults in management concealed'.

Such an attack on the Company, even though it was a reprint from another journal, was almost unprecedented in Swindon. Sir Daniel Gooch, the Chairman of the G.W.R. Company, was also criticised locally, for his opposition to the proposed Swindon, Marlborough and Andover Railway, and his refusal to allow the new line to use the Junction Station. However, the line to Marlborough was opened in July 1881, the journey, via Ogbourne and Chiseldon taking 35 minutes. A return ticket to Savernake Forest cost 1/-. By 1883 the line was open to Andover, and for 'financial and other reasons', the railway was renamed the Midland and South Western Junction Railway. The Great Western Railway was not very cooperative, and although it did eventually give permission for the Junction Station to be used by the new line, it made further difficulty over the use of its line between Hungerford and Marlborough. By the end of 1883 the M. & S.W. Jct. Railway ran from Cricklade to Andover. Its route was picturesque and delightful, running through the Wiltshire Downs, with small stations and halts set in rich and verdant country. From Swindon Junction the trains travelled to Swindon Town station via

Rice, Samuel, 28, Cromwell-street
Rice, John, 6, Ashburne-terrace, Rodbourne-road
Rich, Mrs. Ann, 8, Kingsdowne-terrace, Clifton-street, King's-hill
Rich, John, 60, Mill-street
Richards, William, 21, Villet-street
Richards, Samuel, 10, Taunton-street
Richards, John, 6, Oxford-street
Richards, Richard, 10, Oxford-street
Richards, W., 52, Clifton-street, King's-hill
Richards, John, 6, Harding-street
Richards, William, 60, William-street
Richards, Thomas, 41, Reading-street
Richardson, James, 3, Havelock-street
Richardson, John, 52, Mill-street
Richens, Martha, 66, Mill-street
Richens, Charles, 6, Mill-street
Richens, James, 7, Edgware-road
Richens, William, 25, Rusbey-place
Richens, Weston, shopkeeper, 16, Gloucester-st.
Ricks, Richard, 30, Westcott-place
Ricks, Charles, 4, College-street
Riddiford, C. D., Maitland-cottage, Bridge-street
Riley, Edwin Charles, 1, Church-place
Ring, W. H. Dixon-street
Ring, William, 47, Regent-street
Rixon, Robert W., 18, Gloucester-street
Rixon, Wm. 2, Ladd's-mill-cottages
Roach, James, 5, Cromwell-street
Roberts, John, 8, Carfax-street
Roberts, Thomas, Clifton-villas
Roberts, T., Clifton-terrace, King's-hill
Roberts, Edward, 7, Ashburne-terrace, Rodbourne-road
Roberts, John, 53, Wellington-street
Robertson, John, 7, Cross-street
Robinson, Benjamin, 1, Henry-street
Robinson, George, 32, Bath-street
Robinson, Joseph, 9, Faringdon-street
Robinson, John, 1, Page-street
Robinson, Kirby, 4, Andover-street
Robinson, John, 6, Westcott-place
Robinson, Wm. 43, Princes-street
Robins, William, 16, Sanford-street
Robins, Isaac, 53, Cheltenham-street
Robins, Thomas, 49, Reading-street
Robbins, A., King's-hill Co-operative, 1, Cambria-bridge-road
Robson, Geoffrey, 27, Reading-street
Robson, Robert T., 75, Redcross-street
Rogers, Mrs. Mary, 3, Farnsby-street
Rogers, Frank, 17, Read-street
Rogers, S., 3, Gloucester-terrace
Rogers, Samuel, 11a, Eastcott-terrace
Rogers, Thomas, 32, Catherine-street
Rolfe, Henry, 2, Sanford-street
Rollin, William, 28, Fleet-street
Rollin, James, 8, London-street
Romans, Wm. 22, Eastcott-hill
Roe, Thomas, 11, Faringdon-street
Roe, James, 2, Cambria-place
Roser, George, 1, Haydon-street
Rowe, Francis, 15, Taunton-street
Rowe, Patrick, 34, Bath-street
Rowe, W., 31, Oxford-street
Rowland, George, baker, 2, Rusbey-place
Rowland, Edwin, 39, Bath-street
Rowland, John, 14, Albion-street
Rowland, Eli, 4, Regent-place
Rowland, Thomas, 7, Cetus-buildings
Rowland, William, 25, Farnsby-street
Rowney, Thomas, 10, Westcott-place
Ruddle, Henry, 35, Princes-street

Ridman, W., 4, Jacob-terrace
Rushton, Richard, Queen's-Arms-hotel, Station
Rumings, John, 3, Havelock-street
Rushton, John, King-street
Rushdown, George, 17, King-street
Russel, Frederick Henry, 26, Cheltenham-street
Russel, Charles, 7, King-street
Russell, John, 57, Princes-street
Russell, James, 25, Bath-street
Ryan, Bartholomew, 5, Hay-lane-cottages
Ryland, George, 18, Carronel
Rymill, James, 24, Wellington-place
Sainsbury, Wm. 60, Clifton-street, King's-hill
Sainsbury, Samuel, 64, Mill-street
Salmon, George W. H., accountant, 14, North-st.
Sambrook, David, 52, Exeter-street
Sambrook, Benjamin, 50, Bath-street
Sandey, John, 51, Albion-street
Sandey, Henry, tailor, 7, Carlton-street
Saunders, Mary S., Princes-street
Saunders, John, 50, Princes-street
Saunder, Alfred, 70, Eastcott-hill
Saunder, Henry, 12, Haydon-street
Saunders, Chas. 12, John-street
Saunders, George, 26, Haydon-street
Saunders, Thos. 6, Cetus-buildings
Sawyer, George, Hanford-villas, 3, Rolleston-street
Sawyer, Wm. 19, Eastcott-hill
Sawyer, Thomas, 27, Princes-street
Saxton, Frederick, plasterer, 7, Mill-street
Saxten, Thomas D., 22, Clifton-street, King's-hill
Schmitz, H., watchmaker, 87, Regent-street
Schofield, John, 28, Cheltenham-street
Scofield, John, Alvescott-house, 10, Eastcott-hill
Scott, George, 27, Sheppard-street
Seager, James, 2, Hay-lane-cottages
Seager, Frederick, Henry, 61, Medgbury-road
Sealey, Henry, 12, Holbrook-road
Seaton, William, 61, Princes-street
Selby, Richard, 24, Gooch-street
Selby, Maurice, 8, Brunel-street
Selby, Thomas, 44, Eastcott-hill
Selwood, Henry, 24, Brunel-street
Sexton, George, 26, Albion-street
Sexton, John, 60, Eastcott-hill
Seymour, John, grocer, 14, Eastcott-hill
Shackle, Wm. 31, Redcross-street
Shackle, George, 33, Westcott-place
Shail, Stephen, 10, Sanford-street
Shail, George, Foresters Arms-inn, 15, Fleet-st.
Shail, James, 41, Westcott-place
Shakspeare, James, 14, Mill-street
Shalivoff, Samuel, 17, Harding-street
Shannon, Henry, 11, Rolleston-street
Sharman, Mrs. 65, Clifton-street, King's-hill
Sharpe, Mrs. 28, Prospect-hill
Sharpe, W., 15, Stafford-street
Sharp, Stephen, 44, Eastcott-hill
Sharp, John, 52, Mill-street
Shaw, Francis, 10, Page-street
Shaw, John Thomas, 45, Westcott-place
Shearman, Mrs. 14, Cheltenham-street
Sheldon, John Harry, 47, Westcott-place
Sheldon, Mrs. Isabella, 44, Sanford-street
Sheldon, William, 18, College-street
Sheldon, Mrs E., assistant mistress College-street Schools, 4, Sanford-street,
Shell, Charles, 6, Holbrook-street
Shelly, Mrs. Mary, milliner and dressmaker, 34, Bridge-street
Sheppard, Alfred, 7, Harding-street
Sheppard, Mrs. S., 7, Gloucester-terrace
Sheppard, Nelson, 60, Bridge-street
Sheppard, Wm. S., 21, Bath-street
Sheppard, Frederick, 6, Hay-lane-cottages

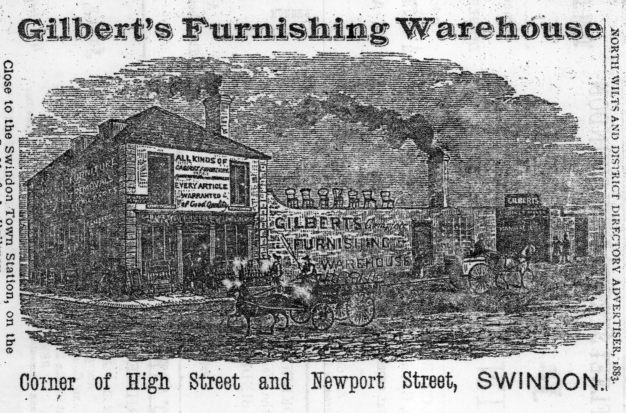

PARLIAMENTARY ELECTION 1886.

Declaration of the Poll, at the Square Old SWINDON.

Candidates, N.Story-Maskelyne,(Elected) B.C.F.Costello,and

Sir John Bennett.

Rushey Platt Junction, running through West Leaze and adjacent to the
present Mill Lane. Leaving Swindon Town Station, (on the south side
of Newport Street), the line ran to Chiseldon, and followed the old
Roman road to Ogbourne and Marlborough.

From Marlborough it ran alongside the famous Savernake Forest to
Savernake Station, and then on to Grafton and Burbage Station. At
Collingbourne it crossed the small River Bourne, and reached Andover
by way of Ludgershall and Weyhill. The engines were small and
friendly, the speed of the trains of a comfortable and leisurely
rate, enabling the passengers to appreciate the ever changing views
of hill and dale, field and wood passing across the windows of the
coaches.

However, the outlook for a 13 year old Swindon boy called Rochester,
was far from pleasant. He had been found guilty of stealing some
gloves from one of the local outfitters, and of re-selling them at a
lower price; his sentence had been one month's imprisonment followed
by 5 years in a reformatory. Morris, in a strongly worded editorial
in the "Advertiser", spoke of a

> shocking sentence on a 13 year old boy, a first
> offender, of respectable parents, condemned to
> spend five years of his youth in the company of
> hardened young criminals, whose influence would
> be bound to do him incalculable harm'.

Unfortunately, Morris's plea for leniency went unanswered.

An incident which caused a great deal of controversy in the town
in 1884 was called by the 'Advertiser' the 'Great Road Case'. The
Lord of the Manor, Ambrose Lethbridge Goddard, had closed the right
of way across the old church road by 'The Planks', and the chorus of
protest came from all quarters of the town. The local authorities sued
the Squire, and the case found its way to Salisbury Assizes, the Judge
being no less a person than the Lord Chief Justice of England. As the
case unfolded it soon became apparent that the Squire would be unable
to justify his action, and he changed his plea to 'Guilty'. Morris
and the Rev. H.G. Baily, the Vicar of Swindon, had been his principal
adversaries, and both seem to have made the most of their victory and
the Squire's discomfiture. This strange case had very little effect

upon the history of the town, but caused so much excitement and anger that it must be mentioned. The Reverend H.G. Baily, who had been Vicar of Swindon since 1843, left the town in 1885 for a quieter living at Lydiard Tregoze. He had been involved in the town's affairs as a church leader and a member of the Old Town Local Board, and Morris, who had on occasions found him a doughty opponent, wrote in appreciative terms of his service to the town. 1885 was an election year and Story-Maskelyne retained his seat with a confortable victory over W. Stone, the Conservative candidate.

There was yet another election in 1886. The Liberal Party was split over the Irish question into three groups - Gladstone Liberals, Liberal Unionists and Parnellites. The confusion was so great that many of the electors at Swindon were not clear on the issues at stake, or of the differences between the candidates. Story-Maskelyne was a Liberal-Unionist, and as such, came in for a lot of criticism from the local press. He was a scientist, a grandson of an Astronomer Royal, and Morris alluded to him as 'the distinguished Professor of dull and lumbering speeches'. The other two candidates were Sir John Bennett and B.F.C. Costello - an 'Irish American Roman Catholic lawyer with an American wife', as he was described. Despite all the abuse that was heaped on him Story-Maskelyne again topped the poll.

A more important matter for the town was the opening of the famous Severn Tunnel in January 1886, for the passage of goods and mineral traffic. This increased the importance of Swindon as a railway junction. The construction of the tunnel had been an immense task; several times flooding had washed away the labour of months and caused loss of life, and its completion was welcomed with relief. Passenger trains began using the tunnel in December 1886. The M.S.W.J. Railway, although still handicapped by the G.W.R.'s lack of cooperation, was running trains through to Portsmouth by 1886.

On 21st June 1887 Swindon celebrated the Golden Jubilee of Queen Victoria. The streets and buildings in the town 'presented a gay and animated appearance, business premises were festooned with decorations, and banners bearing the message "God bless the Queen" were stretched across the streets'. At night rows of burning gas jets illuminated the town.

On the same day the foundation stone of the Victoria Hospital was laid by Charlotte, the wife of A.L. Goddard, the Lord of the Manor, who had donated the land for the building. The old Squire freely admitted that he had wanted to charge the Council £320 for the plot, and had only changed his mind and made it a gift at the insistence of his son. Morris, in his report of the ceremony in the 'Advertiser', gave considerable prominence to this admission.

Wombwells Circus visited the town in July, and the high spot of its visit must have been the daring exploit of

'Mr. G.R. Henley, a local builder, who entered the lions cage, in company with Madam Salva, a woman of colour and an experienced lion tamer, and stayed in there with the lions, for some time. This was a bold feat for a stranger to perform, and on walking out of the cage, Mr. Henley was loudly cheered'.

Across the years, we too, may add our valedictory cheers for this intrepid Daniel of 1887.

In the same year Richard Jefferies, who was born and bred at Coate, died in London. He wrote several magnificent books on the Wiltshire countryside, and his 'Bevis, the story of a boy', has become a classic among books on nature and rural life.

Sir Daniel Gooch, whose name will always be associated with the early days of the G.W.R. and Swindon Works, died in 1889. By then, the small railway settlement of 1841, surrounded by 'green fields', that he and Brunel had chosen, had grown into a huge Works employing thousands of workers; the 'green fields' of which he had written, had long since disappeared, and in their place stood row after row of workshops, filled with machines and engines of massive and intricate design.

For many years after his death this famous Works, in the founding of which he had played so prominent a part, would continue to grow and to produce the renowned locomotives of the Great Western Railway, the 'Stars' and the 'Saints', the 'Castles' and the 'Kings';

locomotives of power and grace that would win the admiration and affection of all who saw them.

Politics, national and local, played a prominent part in the life of the town during the last decade of the century. In addition to four Parliamentary Elections, there were Wilts County Council elections, Local Board elections and elections for the School Board. The inhabitants seem to have had election addresses waved in front of them almost continuously. The Parliamentary Election campaigns did not have the cut and thrust or the excitement that enlivened the earlier contests. One possible reason for this was that Trade Unionism was becoming more prominent, and many of the workmen were more interested in its growth as an organised force than they were in party politics. The amalgamation of the towns and the creation of a Borough of Swindon had also become an important issue.

One voice that would no longer be heard in this and other controversy was that of William Morris, the Proprietor and Editor of the 'Swindon Advertiser' since its inception in 1854. This old campaigner, who for many years had been one of the chief figures on the Swindon scene, involved in every aspect of the developing town, and always ready to speak out against anything that seemed to him to be an injustice, died at Bournemouth in June 1891. He had inevitably made many enemies, and some of his campaigns were rejected by the public, but he had the zeal and energy of a reformer and never gave up. He summed up his own philosophy in an editorial of 1886, in which he stated that since he had been Editor of the 'Advertiser' he had tried to ensure that in the policy of the paper

'we have never trimmed the sails of our barque to
catch a fleeting advantage, we have never shirked
a duty when called upon to perform it'.

Like Stevenson's Alan Breck he was a 'bonny fighter'.

On 2nd October 1891 the new Town Hall was opened. It was at first known as the 'new public offices building', but there was a general anticipation that the creation of a Borough of Swindon could not be long delayed, and that the new building would become the Town Hall. Because of the rapid development of the town there were so many new

Town Hall, Regent Circus, built 1891

Baptist Tabernacle, built 1886

buildings etc., being opened that the authorities had become expert in making the necessary arrangements; the degree of ceremony being adjusted to the importance of the occasion. The Town Hall opening was considered an event of the first importance, worthy of special treatment. The Marquess of Bath agreed to officially declare the building open, and the inhabitants of the town and the owners of business premises were asked, by announcements in the 'Advertiser' and 'North Wilts Herald', to 'decorate their houses and shops with arches, flags and bunting'. A procession through the streets of the town was arranged. The route chosen was Wood Street - High Street - Newport Street - Devizes Road - Bath Road - The Sands - Clifton Street - Radnor Street - Cambria Bridge Road - Faringdon Road - Bridge Street - Regent Street - Regent Circus. Even with the encouragement of the military band some of the more portly civic dignitaries must have been glad when the march was over.

The opening ceremony went very well at the start, but the weather intervened at the climax of the proceedings and the Noble Marquis, the Town Clerk and the assembled notabilities were forced by a heavy thunderstorm to retreat to the shelter of the building. The various contingents outside, including the military band, and the hundreds of spectators and visitors all seem to have got very wet indeed.

The new G.W.R. Baths were opened in 1892, the Telephone Exchange and the County Ground in 1893, and the Town Gardens in 1894. The County Ground was, and still is, an outstanding sports area, with a large cricket ground, surrounded by a cycle track, and complete with an imposing Victorian pavilion, whilst standing adjacent was the famous football ground, the home of Swindon Town Football Club. The Duke of Beaufort had promised to open the Ground, but later withdrew at very short notice, a circumstance that needed lengthy and tortuous explanations from his apologists at the Opening Day luncheon. A Sports Meeting was held to celebrate the opening on 13th May 1893; the weather was perfect, and the only slight disappointment to the hundreds of spectators was that the famous Kibblewhite, a local runner of outstanding ability, was off form and failed to win the Mile.

In the next few years discussion about the amalgamation of Old and New Swindon was almost continuous. There were Parliamentary Elections in 1895, 1898 and 1900, the two main parties remaining more or less in balance. In 1897 the Diamond Jubilee of Queen Victoria was celebrated in the town with patriotic fervour and affectionate respect. Politicians might come and go, elections be won or lost, and a whole way of life be changed, as, indeed, it had been in Swindon, but the Queen remained, unchanged in a changing world.

The Boer War commenced in October 1899, and, as ever, some of the young men volunteered to join up and march away. One who didn't come back was 22 year old L/Corporal E. Henley, who was shot through the head by a Boer sharpshooter at the Modder River - a long way away from his modest home at 10 Byron Street, Swindon.

On 22nd January 1900, the Charter of Incorporation, signed by the Queen, was received in Swindon, and on 9th November the town officially became the Borough of Swindon. It was to be the last Borough that the Queen was ever to create, for on 22nd January 1901 her long reign came to an end. "Our Queen is Dead" ran the headline in the local paper, and as the news was passed quietly around, the people of The Railway Town heard the slow tolling of the bells of Christ Church and St. Mark's echoing through the wintry air.

EPILOGUE

The two gate pillars in High Street, that in 1840 marked the entrance to "The Lawn", the ancestral home of the Goddards, are still standing, graffiti sprayed, although the lodges that flanked them have long since disappeared. The pleasant tree lined avenue that led to the parkland is still there, but "The Lawn" has gone and the old parish church of Holy Rood lies in well kept ruin. From the high ground of the park a fine view of the countryside can still be seen, but the fields and trees that stretched as far as the eye could see have disappeared, and in their place, from east to west, and from the near distance to the horizon, lies the industrial town of Swindon.

To the east of this panorama can be seen the large housing estates of Park, Covingham, Nythe and Dorcan, built to accommodate the Londoners and others who moved to Swindon after 1950, in what has been called the 'second expansion of Swindon'. Across the Stratton road is one of the first factories to come to the town during that time - The Pressed Steel Car Body Works.

Looking north the floodlighting pylons of the Swindon Town Football Club stand out clearly, as does the County Cricket Ground and the red brick factory of the Wills Tobacco Company. Beyond these, and stretching to the horizon are the older estates of Gorse Hill, Pinehurst and Penhill, and to the north west Moredon, Haydon Wick and Rodbourne Cheney. Looking westwards, the green of Queens Park gives a touch of colour, and makes a pleasant foreground to the large and modern buildings that ring the shopping and business centre of the town. The Murray John Building, the Police Headquarters, Hambros, Debenham's, the Wiltshire Hotel and others form a massive concrete barrier that prevents any further view of the old part of the town in general, and in particular, of the British Rail Engineering Works, which occupies the buildings and workshops of the former G.W.R. Locomotive Works. The old G.W.R. Carriage and Wagon Works has largely disappeared, its workshops demolished, and the few remaining buildings occupied by a variety of small industrial firms.

In Swindon, as in Xanadu, a stately pleasure dome has been decreed, and "The Oasis" now stands where the old Wheel and Stamping Shops once stood. The bright lights of the swimming pool and the sound of childrens' laughter has replaced the red glare of the furnaces and the dull, earth shaking thuds of the steam hammers. The North Star Technical College now occupies the land where once stood the old carriage repair shops and sidings. Where once there were 14,000 railway workers there are now, perhaps, 3,000. The huge steam locomotives that were 'Swindon Built', and the pride of the town, have, with a few exceptions, long since been scrapped. The Age of Steam has disappeared, and with it the pre-eminent position of the Railway Works.

Yet, although this has happened, the influence of the railway is still felt in the town. Not only at the British Rail Engineering Works, where 'the pride in the job' of the old railwaymen still persists, but also in a more general way. Many of the hotels and public houses bear names of a railway significance such as "The Locomotive", "The Steam Train", or "The Rolling Mills". Many of the streets are named after railway notabilities. There is a large and popular Railway Museum, and the Swindon Health Centre is housed in the old G.W.R. Medical Fund building. Even the new estates and factories that have come to the town may indirectly owe their existence to the railway.

It was through its Railway Works that Swindon became known throughout the country as an engineering town, and its mechanics and workers had a high reputation. The products of their labour and skill were to be seen by any traveller on the G.W.R. Consequently, when the second expansion of Swindon began many firms were attracted to the town because they felt there would be a supply of skilled labour available to run their factories.

In the centre of the town a multi million pound covered complex of shops, stores and arcades has been built. It has been named the "Brunel Centre", and a life sized statue of the great engineer dominates the main approach. He gazes ahead in timeless meditation, oblivious of the hurrying crowds, or the young people who sit at his feet and scrawl strange slogans and messages on the stone pedestal on which he stands.

The naming of the Centre, and the statue of the man who, way back in 1840, brought the G.W.R. to Swindon is a pleasing acknowledgement of the importance the town attaches to its railway past. There were others, too, who played their part in the making of that past, and after raising a respectful eye to the great man, we turn, and through the mists of time, see them pass.

First comes young Daniel Gooch, who shared the famous picnic lunch with Brunel, and picked the place whereon to build the Works, then Ambrose Goddard and his son Ambrose Lethbridge Goddard, Lords of the Manor of Swindon, followed by the unknown driver that saved the runaway train. Poor Barbara Patterson and little Miss Thomson, the seamstress of the Railway Village, are followed by Morris of 'The Advertiser', still debating a forgotten cause. Piper and Cadogan come next, their differences resolved, and Richard Jefferies, still dreaming of the fields and lake of Coate.

Armstrong and Dean bring on the railway workers, who give a cheer for the Boer War volunteers, marching in step to a military band. The crowd thickens and the Swindonians of 1840-1901 - our forbears of 'The Railway Town' - pass by. As the strains of "Soldiers of the Queen" fade and die, we raise our hand in salute, and L/Corporal Henley turns and waves his last goodbye.

Appendix 1

The population growth of Swindon
1841-1901

Year	New Swindon	Old Swindon	Total
1841	--	2459	2459
1851	2300	2576	4876
1861	4167	2689	6856
1871	7628	4092	11720
1881	15086	4818	19904
1891	27295	5544	32839
1901			44996

Source: Home Office Census Returns

Appendix 2

Church and School Building in Swindon
1840-1901

Until the coming of the railway there was only one church in Swindon, namely, the parish church of Holy Rood, dating from 1154, and, according to some authorities, possibly before that date. With the building of the Railway Village another church became necessary and St. Mark's was built in 1845. Holy Rood was structurally unsound and too small and in 1851 a new parish church was built in Cricklade Street and named Christ Church. Five of the Holy Rood church bells (dated 1741) were transferred to Christ Church, where they still form part of the peal. The tower clock, dating from 1843, was also removed to Christ Church where it still keeps good time.

In the 1870's the town began to expand north of the railway line in the Gorse Hill and Rodbourne areas, and mission churches were built to meet the spiritual needs of the people. St. Barnabas's church began in a temporary building in Gorse Hill in 1874, but it was not until 1885 that the present church was built. As the New Town developed the pressure on St. Mark's grew, and to relieve this pressure a new church, St. Paul's, was built in 1881. In 1883 another daughter church of St. Mark's, St. John's, was built to meet the needs of the rapidly developing Queenstown district of the parish. St. Saviour's (1890) was built to serve the south western corner of the parish. This church was built by the voluntary labour of the parishioners, many of whom were employed in the G.W.R. Works.

A Roman Catholic mission met once a month at the Greyhound Inn in Westcott Place in 1848, and in 1851 a Roman Catholic chapel was opened on a site between Bridge Street and Sanford Street. A Roman Catholic church of Holy Rood was opened in 1882.

There had been several sporadic attempts to introduce Methodism into Swindon before the coming of the railway, and meetings were held in a number of humble cottages in Eastcott Hill. In 1849 the first Primitive

Methodist chapel was opened in Regent Street. It was completely rebuilt in 1863. By 1875 the chapel was again found to be too small and in the following year a third chapel was built on the site. During the last twenty years of the 19th century five new Primitive Methodist chapels were built.

A Congregational chapel existed in Newport Street in 1804. A breakaway group from this chapel formed the nucleus of the Particular Baptist congregation for whom a chapel was built in South Street in 1845. The Newport Street chapel flourished and in 1866 a new chapel was built at the corner of Bath Road and Victoria Street. In 1877 an iron chapel was erected in Sanford Street.

A Wesleyan Methodist chapel in 'The Planks', built prior to the arrival of the railway, was pulled down in 1862, and a new octagonal one, with seating for 300, erected on the same site. This chapel served the Wesleyan Methodists in Swindon until 1880, when a new and more imposing chapel with accommodation for 600, was built at Bath Road. The second Wesleyan chapel, the first in New Town, was built in Bridge Street. In 1858 this chapel was pulled down and a larger one built in nearby Faringdon Road. In 1869 this chapel was also demolished and a large building in Faringdon Road known as 'The Barracks' was converted into a chapel and remained as such until 1959. The Wesleyan Methodists also built Mission Halls at Gorse Hill in 1871, and Percy Street in 1877. Like the Primitive Methodists the Wesleyans were particularly active during the period 1881-1900 and four new chapels were opened.

The first Baptist chapel was built at Fleet Street and opened in 1849, whilst the Welshmen and their families who came to Swindon in the 1860's when the Rail Mill in the G.W.R. Works was opened, had their own Cambria Bridge Chapel built in 1866. In 1886 the Baptists built their imposing Tabernacle in Regent Street, with seating for 1,000.

In 1840 there were seven schools in Swindon but only one of them - The National School in Newport Street - was a free school. The others were fee paying schools or 'academies' with the pupils being the children of the local gentry or the more well to do tradesmen.

The arrival of the G.W.R. workers and their families in 1843 created a demand for schooling that could not be satisfied by the existing schools in Old Town, and in 1845 the G.W.R. Company opened its own school in Bristol Street. The school was primarily intended for children of G.W.R. employees, and was supervised by the Company, but children of parents not connected with the G.W.R. were admitted for a fee of 1/- per week. In 1858 a local committee took over the supervision of the school, and within a few years it became apparent that the building was too small to meet the demand for places. In 1871 the school had 700 pupils, and in 1874 the girls were moved to a new school in College Street.

Other schools in the town by 1870 were the National School in Victoria Street (120 girls), the old National School in Newport Street (120 boys), and various schools associated with religious denominations, such as the Wesleyan Day School (100 mixed), the New Congregational Church and School in Victoria Street (80 mixed), the Eastcott Church of England School (55 mixed), and the Primitive Methodist School for girls.

However, the growth of the town was so rapid that these schools could not provide sufficient places for the increasing number of children. In the spring of 1871 700 to 800 children were not being taught because of this situation, and as a temporary measure the New Town Drill Hall was used to accommodate some of these children. In June 1877 a public meeting was held, and a decision taken to implement a common policy in juvenile education for New and Old Swindon. This rapidly brought results and in the next few years Gorse Hill School (1878), Queenstown (1880), Westcott (1878), Gilbert's Hill (1880) and Even Swindon (1880) opened. In 1878 the first Roman Catholic school was opened.

As the town grew in the 1880's and 90's so new schools were built. Sanford Street Boys (1881) was followed by Clifton Street Mixed (1884), Lethbridge Road Mixed (1891) and Clarence Street Mixed in 1897. A school was built at Rodbourne Cheney in 1892 and a Higher Grade Education

day school was opened in the newly built Victoria Road Technical Institute.

In addition to the Board Schools there were many private schools, some of the more prominent being Reverend R. Breeze's Academy (1856), the George Nourse Academy in Victoria Street (1856), Mr. and Mrs. Steger's Mixed School in the Market Place (1857), Miss Cowell's School for Young Ladies in Devizes Road (1858), Miss Sykes's School in Fleetway Terrace (1861), Miss Murdoch's Ladies School at 2 Taunton Street (1865), J.B. Bowles's School at Belle View House (1856) and Mr. Snell's High School for Boys in Bath Road. The High School is still in use as a school, although it has now been renamed.

Appendix 3

The Arms of Swindon

On the 22nd January, 1900, Her Majesty Queen Victoria granted a Charter of Incorporation by which Swindon became a municipal borough. Almost at once consideration was given to the need for Borough Arms, and a competition was announced for the submitting of designs. A Committee sat on the 18th March 1901 to consider the designs and of those submitted two were chosen. The College of Arms finally submitted a design which incorporated elements from both designs, and this final version was accepted by the Committee on the 27th June 1901. At the same meeting it was agreed that the motto should be Salubritas et Industria (Health and Industry) and that the Mayor be requested to furnish a correct drawing of a modern G.W.R. locomotive for the use of the Heralds' College. It would seem that the drawing submitted was that of 'White Horse', a 4-2-2 class locomotive constructed in 1891. The actual document granting the arms to the Borough is dated 23rd September 1901.

The shield is quartered in alternate colours of blue and red, and divided horizontally by a wavy line. In the first quarter a silver pile bears three red crescents. In the second quarter are three silver castles. The third quarter contains a golden mitre. On the upper third of the shield stands a locomotive in natural colours on a silver background, the whole surmounted by a crest consisting of a bent forearm grasping two golden hammers crossed above a wreath in silver and blue.

The winged wheel represents New Swindon in its provision of swift travel by means of the railway.

The Strong Arm and crossed hammers may be taken to illustrate the motto, Health and Industry.

The helmet surmounting the shield indicates the rank of the person or persons to whom the arms have been granted. There are four degrees and the helmet shown on the Swindon Arms is of the fourth and last degree, namely gentlemen and esquires.

The Four Quarters doubly represent 'Old' and 'New' Swindon.

The Three Crescents are from the arms of the Goddard family who held the Manor of Swindon from 1560 and were closely associated with the development of Old Swindon.

The Three Castles are from the arms of the Vilett family who, from the 17th century, held the Manor on which New Swindon has grown.

The Mitre represents Odo, Bishop of Bayeux, to whom William I gave Old Town in 1066, as recorded in the Domesday Book.

Appendix 4

Maps of Swindon

1826   Swindon before the arrival of the railway.

1850   The arrival of the railway and the building of the
        Locomotive Works - building of the Railway Village
        and settlements in the Westcott area.

1883   General development of New Swindon and Prospect area.

1889   Development in Theobald Street, Chester Street and
        Faringdon Road area - Victoria Hospital built - Kent
        Road estate being developed - Victoria Road further
        developed - building of Avenue Road and Lethbridge
        Road.

1894   Gorse Hill and Rodbourne developed - Rolleston estate
        laid out and being completed - County Ground and Town
        Gardens opened - Park Lane, George Street, Butterworth
        Street area developed - further building in Clifton
        and Exmouth Street area - Town Hall (Public Offices)
        built and Regent Circus developed.

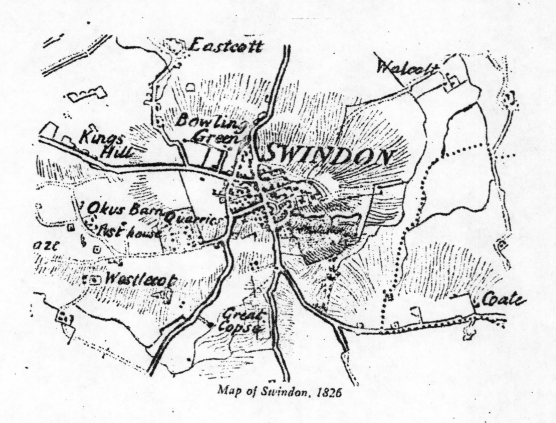

Map of Swindon, 1826

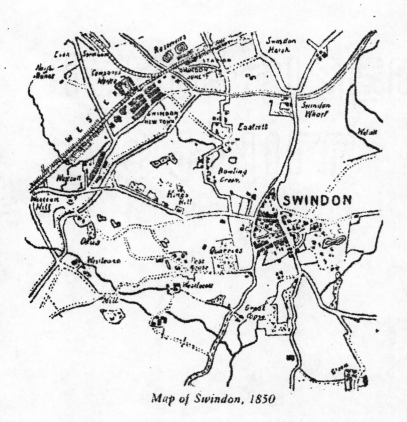

Map of Swindon, 1850

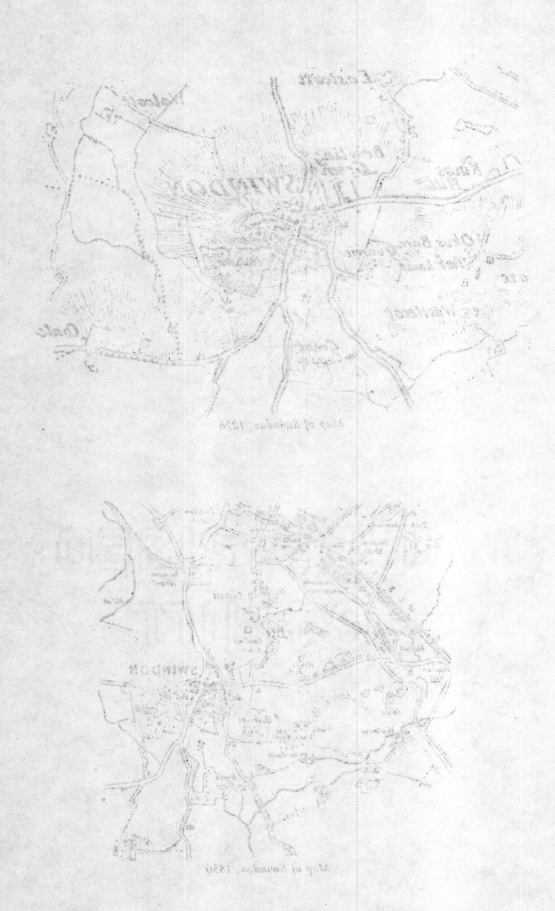

Map of Swindon, 1826

Map of Swindon, 1850

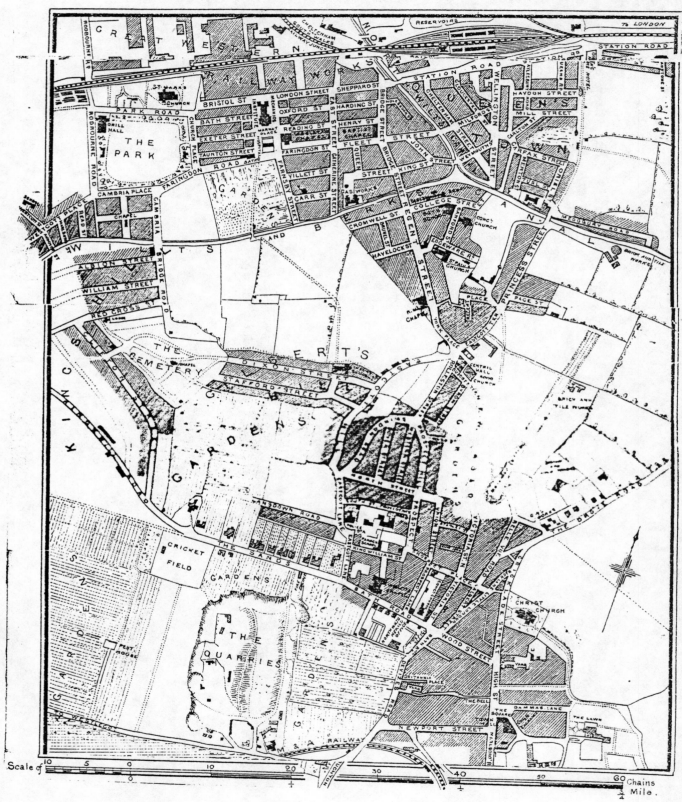

MAP OF SWINDON 1883

MAP OF SWINDON 1889

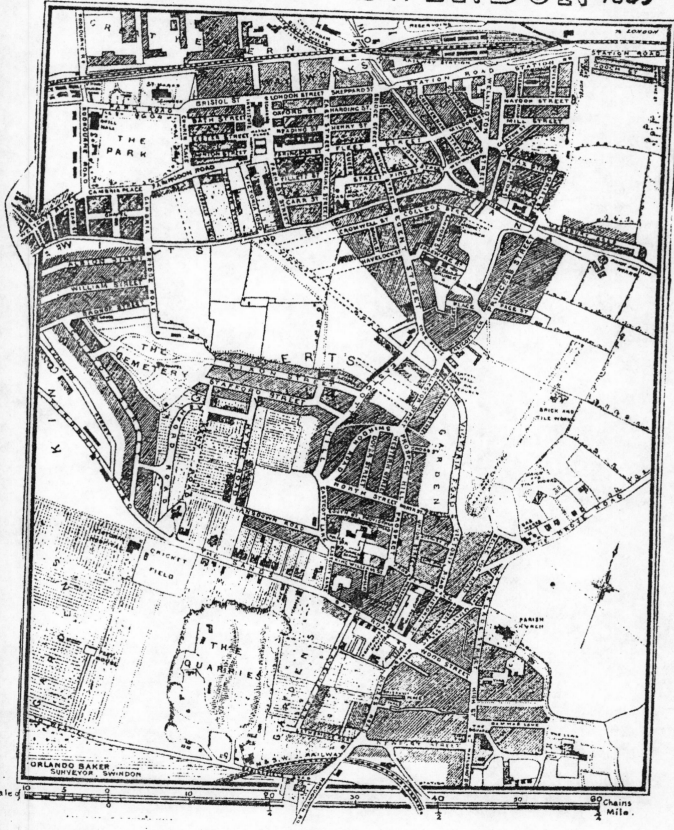

ORLANDO BAKER
SURVEYOR, SWINDON

MAP OF SWINDON

1894

New Swindon Recreation Ground.

Gorse Hill

G.W.R. (Main Line)

To Highworth

Wilts County Ground.

Great Western Railway Works

Swindon Marsh Farm

Cemetery

Church Farm

Cricket Field.

Lower Walcot

Park Farm.

West Leaze

Midland & South Western Junction Railway

To Devizes

To Marlborough

Select Bibliography

There is a very wide collection of works on Wiltshire, Swindon and the
G.W.R. available at the Archives and Reference Department of Swindon
Public Library, and most of the material in Sections 1, 2 and 3 has
been obtained from this source. Students and others interested in local
history will find the microfilm copies of the "Swindon Advertiser" and
the "North Wilts Herald" invaluable for giving a background picture of
life in the town. There is a large number of old photographs available,
and the collection of books on the Steam Locomotive must be one of the
finest in the country. In addition to the selection of Pamphlets and
Articles given in Section 3, readers will find many more at the Library,
and are especially recommended to the 'Wiltshire Pamphlets' collection.

Mr. J.A. Gould's collection of Swindon memorabilia and Mr. Alan
Lenham's items, particularly those on Swindon Cricket, have been made
available to me, and I am grateful to these gentlemen for giving me the
benefit of their wide knowledge of the local history of the town. The
Swindon Society, which meets once monthly and welcomes new members, has
available much valuable information, not only in its large collection
of material and photographs, but also in the collective knowledge of its
members. Membership details are available at the Reference Library.

Section 1 - MS Sources

Chart recording names and addresses of occupants of Swindon Railway
Village 1843.
Manager's Order Book of G.W.R. Swindon Works 1850-1889.
Minutes of the proceedings of Swindon New Town Local Board 1864-1900.
Minutes of the proceedings of Swindon Old Town Local Board 1864-1900.
Minutes of meetings of Newport Street Congregational Chapel 1840-1850.

Section 2 - Printed Documentary Material

Commercial Directory of Wiltshire, ed. J. Robson, 1838.

G.W.R. Mechanics' Institute Library Catalogues 1877-1901.

Kelly's Directory of Wilts, 1800.

North Wilts Directories, 1885-1900.

Swindon Almanack and Parish Register, ed. W. Dore 1864.

Swindon and District Directories, ed. W. Astill, 1879, 1881, 1883.

Vox Stellarum or a Loyal Almanack, ed. F. Moore, 1852, 1855, 1856, 1858, 1860-65, 1868.

Report of Board of Health Inspector, on Swindon, 1850.

Text of Riot Act read by Superintendent George North at Swindon.

Parliamentary Election, 1880.

The Parliamentary Gazetteer of England and Wales 1840-1843. (A. Fullerton and Co. London 1843).

"Swindon Advertiser", 1854-1901 (Microfilm).

"North Wilts Herald", 1861-1901 (Microfilm).

Section 3 - Pamphlets and Articles

Chambers Edinburgh Journal 13th August 1853. "Swindon and the Broad Gauge". (Anon.)

G.W.R. Company "Swindon Works 1892". (Pamphlet dated 1893).

"The Town and Works of Swindon". (1892).

"Swindon Works 1898".

Swindon Advertiser 28th September 1928. "Looking back on the history of Swindon". (article by R. George).

The Sphere 6th November 1965. "The British locomotive industry". (Article by C.D. Woodward).

Transport History 1967 "The early days of the railway community of Swindon". (Article by K. Hudson).

University of Birmingham Historical Journal 1955. "The G.W.R. and Swindon Works in the Great Depression". (Article by D.E.C. Eversley).

Wiltshire Archaeological and Natural History Magazine 1861. "Swindon and its neighbourhood". (Article by J.E. Jackson).

Section 3 - Pamphlets and Articles (contd.)

<u>Wiltshire Life</u> December 1965. "Wiltshire Towns now and then - Swindon". (Article by P.S. Fry).

<u>Wiltshire Pamphlets</u> - Swindon Reference Library.

Section 4 - General Works

Averies, S.J.	<u>Regent Street Methodist Church 1849-1949</u>. (Swindon 1950).
Aubrey, J.	<u>A Natural History of Wiltshire</u> ed. D. Britten (London 1890).
Bearn, R.	<u>The Catholic Church in Swindon</u> (Swindon 1960)
Best, G.	<u>Mid-Victorian Britain</u>. (Weidenfeld and Nicolson).
Bird, Denis.	<u>The Story of Holy Rood</u>. (Swindon 1975).
Child, Mark.	<u>Aspects of Swindon History</u>. (Swindon 1969).
Dalby, L.J.	<u>The Wilts and Berks Canal</u>. (The Oakwood Press).
Darwin, B.	<u>A century of Medical Service, the story of the G.W.R. Medical Fund 1847-1947</u> (Swindon 1948).
Evans, Joan.	<u>The Victorians</u>. (Cambridge University Press).
Gooch, Sir Daniel.	<u>The diaries of Sir Daniel Gooch</u>. (Keegan, Paul).
Grindsell, L.V.)	
Wells, H.B.)	
Tallamy, H.S.)	<u>Studies in the history of Swindon.</u>
Betjeman, John)	(Swindon 1950)
Harrison, J.F.C.	<u>The early Victorians 1832-1851</u>. (Weidenfeld and Nicolson).
Herbert, Christopher	<u>A Social History of Victorian England</u>. (Oxford University Press).
Jefferies, R.	<u>Jefferies Land, A History of Swindon and its environs</u>. ed. Grace Toplis. (London 1882) <u>The Hills and the Vales</u>. (London 1882)
Large, F.	<u>A Swindon Retrospect</u>. (Swindon 1892)
Lloyd, J.D.	<u>The development of Education in Swindon</u>. (Bristol University M.A. Thesis 1954. Swindon 1969)

Section 4 - General Works (contd.)

Kitson Clark, G.   The makings of Victorian England. (Methuen).

Lindley, K.   Town, Time and People. (Swindon 1969).

McDermot, T.   A History of the Great Western Railway. 3 vols.
(London 1969).

Pudney, John.   Brunel and his World (Thames and Hudson. 1974).

Thompson, Francis   The Collected Poems of Francis Thompson. (Oxford
University Press 1932).

Williams, Alfred.   Life in a Railway Factory. (London 1915).

The Victoria County History of Wilts. Vols. IV and IX. (Oxford University
Press London, 1970).

INDEX

INDEX

INDEX

INDEX